This book, *Protection: Safety and Dominion in Perilous Times* by Dr. Miltenberger can truly teach you how to dwell in safety and have dominion in the perilous times in which we live. These are dangerous times, not only with terrorism in our world, but where people are giving themselves more and more to the influences of darkness in them and choosing to act out from those influences.

As Dr. Miltenberger lays out line upon line we do not have to be affected by these influential forces. We can rise in the power and dominion given to us by Jesus Himself and rule over any weapon the devil tries to use against us. One of the great Psalms of protection in the Bible is Psalm 91. In this literary work the 91st Psalm is masterfully explained with real life testimonies of walking in the deliverance and protection offered to all believers.

As you read this book give careful study and consideration to what is being declared and taught. Meditate on it, keep it in your thinking, mull over it and you will come to the place of faith where you can be continually dwelling in the safety and dominion of Blood Covenant Protection.

DR. BOB RAIMONDO
Senior Pastor
New Life Family Worship
Punta Gorda, Florida

This book is dedicated to Lena, my loving wife and best friend.
You have always encouraged me to never give up and to pursue
excellence and greatness for His glory.

Also, to my precious children Joshua and Hannah,
who have both been such a blessing and brought me so much joy.
I am truly blessed to have such a wonderful and loving family

PROTECTION

Safety and Dominion in Perilous Times

PROTECTION

Safety and Dominion in Perilous Times

DR. BRIAN MILTENBERGER

Harvest International

20 19 18 17   10 9 8 7 6 5 4 3 2 1

Protection: Safety and Dominion in Perilous Times

ISBN 978-1-7325250-6-1

Copyright © 2018 by Brian Miltenberger

CONTENTS

INTRODUCTION

&

The world is in trouble. It seems that everyone agrees with the title of the old R.E.M. song: "It's the End of the World As We Know It." The world knows trouble is coming. Society can sense that something bad is on the horizon. Coyote has caught up with Road Runner and Sylvester is having Tweety Bird for dinner.

Television and movies are inundated with the themes of apocalypse. Everyone, including agnostics, atheists, and even liberal theologians, realizes we are on the brink of disaster. All hell is about to break loose. Time is not slowing down but appears to be speeding up. All around us is crumbling. Those neighborhoods once most safe and influential are now broken down. A wealthy family opens their door to a pizza delivery guy who ends up slaughtering them with a hunter's knife and burning their mansion to the ground. The world is not a safe place to live. The rioting has not ended; it has only just begun. Mother Nature seems to always be having a bad hair day.

Consider these recent headlines:

- "Minnesota teen planned school massacre" (CNN.com, May 2, 2014)
- "3 Dead after Gunman Opens Fire at Louisiana Movie Theater" (CNN.com, July 23, 2015)

- "7.0 Quake strikes Japan; Rescuers Try to Free Residents" (CNN.com, April 16, 2016)

- "Houston flooding: Deaths and more rain to come", " (CNN.com, April 20, 2016)

- "Deadly Tornado Outbreak" (Weather.gov, January 22, 2017)

- "Federal health officials investigating multi-state E. coli outbreak" (ABCNews.com, March 2, 2017)

- "Naked Gunman Kills 4 in Waffle House Shooting" (NPR.org, April 22, 2018)

The media constantly bombards us with bad news about the latest murder, car accident, plane crash, missing child, terrorist threat, mass shooting, life threatening virus, or natural disaster. It seems no place is exempt from danger. There is peril all around. Regardless of where we live on the planet, we are all confronted with extreme violence and chaos.

What are people supposed to do to keep safe? How do you prepare for danger when your child's school has no history of violence? How do you protect yourself when you have little or no warning of impending disaster? How do you know that today you won't be hit by an intoxicated driver or a careless motorist texting while driving? How can you be assured that your family's vacation will not be interrupted by a terrorist attack? Does the airline guarantee your flight will not end up in the ocean? Are your children safe to ride their bicycles around the block, or are they in danger of being snatched by a pedophile? Are you in jeopardy of being killed by a random shooter at the shopping mall this week? Will your children be murdered in a movie theatre?

There is a widespread fear of sudden death, unexpected danger, and unavoidable tragedy. It seems society has become darker and more dangerous than in any previous generation. Satan knows that his time is short and so he has unleashed his wrath on this world. It is essential for you to know that your heavenly Father will protect you from all danger, no matter how dark the world around you may get.

You don't have to live in fear of danger. You can have peaceful assurance of divine protection and longevity of life. There is available to every believer who has faith in Jesus Christ, a blood covenant of divine protection and permanency of life. God intended for you to live your life free from fear, always abiding in His hiding place of protection.

We are living in the last days of dangerous times: "But know this, that in the last days perilous times will come" (2 Timothy 3:1). In these last days, God is revealing to His people how to live free from fear, even though we live in a world full of menace. We can live in a peaceful state of quiet assurance, dwelling safely underneath our Father's protective wings.

Jesus gave us the new covenant perspective of the Father's character and nature when He said He is the good shepherd who will always protect His sheep.

NO ONE LIKES A BULLY

The 1985 movie Back to the Future, tells the story of teenager Marty McFly and his parents, George and Lorraine. In the film, Marty goes back in time to witness events from George and Lorraine's past. Marty watches as the younger version of George is consistently bullied by his high school classmate, Biff. All this comes as no surprise to Marty since in the present, he often sees George being bullied by a now-grown Biff. In the course of the story, high school Biff gets drunk at the school dance and forces himself on Lorraine. The pinnacle of the action occurs when George comes upon Biff and Lorraine in the parking lot, finally musters the courage to stand up to Biff, and rescues his future wife by knocking out the bully. Marty's parents fall in love, George is filled with new courage, and the future is changed. In the revised version of the future, rather than George being a helpless victim of Biff's bullying, George is a successful businessman and the bully Biff is an obsequious auto valet who eagerly maintains and washes George's cars. The future of Marty's family was completely changed because George refused to continue being bullied. No one likes a bully. Everyone wants to see tyranny defeated and the oppressed go free once and for all.

Mouse in the House

When I was in my teens, I was very small for my age. I remember seeing tears in my mother's eyes as she dropped me off to school because she felt sorry for me. My first day at high school, I was asked by teachers if I was lost because they thought I was an elementary school student. They couldn't believe someone who looked so childlike could be a freshman in high school. I was always the short and scrawny one in my class. I was called all kinds of nicknames - Little Man, Runt, BA (from The A Team), Tattoo (from Fantasy Island) - but the one I hated the most was when they called me "Richard Simmons" (surely you remember "Sweatin' to the Oldies"). Needless to say, I was the "mouse in the house." Every day during lunch, I would sit alone and watch the bigger kids play basketball. The only time I got the ball was when someone missed a shot and would yell, "Hey Richard! Get the ball!" I was always on the bench for every sport. I was the little guy no one ever wanted on their team.

Though I was the smallest boy in school, I knew God would keep me safe. Though I couldn't see them, I knew I had angels all around me who were watching over me. I faced those who tried to bully me. I absolutely refused to fear anyone, regardless of their size or threats. I stood toe to toe with anyone who threatened me. I always believed that my Father God was for me and would keep me safe. I refused to tolerate being bullied and always remained safe under the shadow of the Lord's protection.

Face to Face with a Bully

A bully is someone who uses superior strength or influence to intimidate another, typically to force the other person to do what the bully wants. A bully is someone who persecutes, oppresses, tyrannizes, harasses, torments, intimidates, dominates, and pushes others around. Bullying is not just something that happens in the schoolyard. Satan is the chief of all bullies. He bullies you by planting thoughts of fear, hopelessness, sin, and wrong belief in your mind. He wants to intimidate you so he can push you around.

He roars at you in his attempt to make you believe that he can devour you (1 Peter 5:8). The good news is that the enemy cannot touch you if you refuse to let him!

> *But the One Who was begotten of God carefully watches over and protects him [Christ's divine presence within him preserves him against the evil], and the wicked one does not lay hold (get a grip) on him or touch [him].*

> 1 John 5:18, AMPC

When I was in middle school, I came face to face with a bully. I was new to the school and had no friends. One of the boys decided to bully me to show how much bigger and stronger he was. When the teacher left the room, the bully snatched all my belongings and threw them across the classroom. Before I could think, I laid hands on him with the "five-fold ministry" (in other words, I punched him in the face). All the kids were shocked that I stood up to the boy, since he was much bigger then me. After he picked himself up off the ground, he grabbed me by the arms, lifted me off the ground and pinned me against the wall. He then shouted in my face, "I'm gonna kill you – you little runt!" Just at that moment, the teacher walked into the classroom.

You have to understand something about this teacher. He was no ordinary teacher; he was the high school football coach and was very intimidating. He looked like a 500-pound gorilla! He also had a glass eye that he would pull out of its socket so he could polish it during class. The thought of him polishing that eye still gives me chills. He also was the one in charge of giving out the "whacks." For those who may not understand, that means he would spank the misbehaving students with a wooden paddle; he was in charge of administering the corporal punishment. He would motion with his finger to the student who was in trouble and simply say, "Follow me." Everyone dreaded hearing those words from this teacher.

When my teacher walked into the classroom and saw that I was pinned against the wall, he simply motioned with his finger to the bully and said, "Put him down! Follow me!" Later we heard in the distance...Whack! Whack! Whack!

Did you know the Lord will take care of your enemies? You don't have to try to avenge yourself when you are dwelling in the secret place. "Vengeance is Mine, and recompense; their foot shall slip in due time; for the day of their calamity is at hand, and the things to come hasten upon them" (Deuteronomy 32:35).

The Devil's Punisher

Did you know that Jesus is like that big middle school teacher? You see, God is good to us, but He is bad to our adversary. When Jesus defeated Satan at the cross, He became the devil's punisher. We know Jesus as good, but the devil only knows Him as bad. Every time you mention in faith the blood of Jesus, the devil trembles in fear. Jesus, your Lord and Savior, is good all the time to you, but He is bad all the time to the devil.

It didn't matter how big and bad that bully was who pinned me to the wall, the history teacher was much bigger and badder. It's the same with Jesus. The devil is a bully. He will try to fill your mind with fearful thoughts to convince you that he is a lion that is able to devour you, but don't worry. When you receive freely the blood covenant of divine protection, the only thing the devil can do is roar; he cannot devour you, nor can he touch you.

> *Casting all your care upon Him, for He cares for you. Be sober, be vigilant; because your adversary the devil walks about like a roaring lion, seeking whom he may devour.*

1 Peter 5:7-8

Notice, this verse does not say the devil can devour you. It only says that he walks around *seeking* whom he may devour. That means the only way he can devour you is if you let him. He acts like the king of the jungle. The devil is no king, but only the prince of flies (aka Beelzebub). You never have to fear the devil.

He is a liar and a loser. Jesus, the Lion of Judah, knocked out his teeth 2,000 years ago.

> *Arise, O LORD; Save me, O my God! For You have struck all my enemies on the cheekbone; You have broken the teeth of the ungodly. Salvation belongs to the LORD. Your blessing is upon Your people. Selah.*

> Psalm 3:7-8

When you abide underneath the shadow of the wings of the Almighty, the enemy cannot touch you. He may attempt to attack you with thoughts of fear, shame, and blame. Don't let him. Confess boldly that you are washed, forgiven, justified, and protected by the blood of Jesus. Every time you use the Word of God, the name of Jesus, and the blood against the adversary, it's like Jesus himself is grabbing the devil by the nape of the neck and giving him whacks in the hallways of heaven! Jesus is the punisher of all bullies, but it's up to you to not tolerate being bullied any longer.

The Friend of God

When you put your trust in the Lord as your protector, you will discover Him to be a friend who watches over you. "But there is a friend who sticks closer than a brother" (Proverbs 18:24). Abraham was called the friend of God simply because he believed in God: "And the Scripture was fulfilled which says, 'Abraham believed God, and it was accounted to him for righteousness.' And he was called the friend of God" (James 2:23).

When you believe that Jesus is your friend, it causes faith and courage to rise inside you. Believe that Jesus is your friend. He wants to be your BFF – your "best friend forever." You can fearlessly face your adversary knowing that Jesus is your BFF and He has got your back. And if God is for you, who or what can be against you (Romans 8:31)? Identify yourself as God's friend with free access to all Kingdom benefits.

He who did not spare His own Son, but delivered Him up for us all, how shall He not with Him also freely give us all things?

Romans 8:32

Father's Character and Nature

A good father does whatever is necessary to protect the child he loves. That is what our loving heavenly Father has done for us. He saw we were in danger of going to hell, so He sent Jesus, His Son, to pay the penalty for our sins. It is God's will to protect His children not only from an eternal hell, but also from all peril on the earth. Jesus prayed for the Father to keep us from the evil one: "I do not ask that You will take them out of the world, but that You will keep and protect them from the evil one" (John 17:15, AMPC).

The question may arise in your mind, "If God really loves us, then why isn't He protecting everyone?" Someone may answer, "Because God is sovereign and, in His infinite wisdom, works in mysterious ways far above what we can understand." That may sound like a good theological explanation, but it doesn't answer the question. You need to know whether God guarantees you and your family a life of peace, protection, and longevity. You need to know the true character and nature of God, that He is trustworthy and true to His Word.

When our children were young, Lena and I would have someone watch over them when we went out. Before we hired a babysitter, we needed to know their reputation. If the babysitter was known to leave the children unattended for hours with no reasonable explanation for why, we would not entrust our children to that person. We concluded such a babysitter was not trustworthy. If Father God left any of His children in danger, failing to protect them, then we could charge God as untrustworthy. We need to know if God really is a good heavenly Father who is trustworthy, or if He uses His sovereignty as an excuse for negligence.

Father of Light and Life

God does not have any dark side to His nature, and He is not the author of death. He is not teaching us lessons through tragedies and destruction. I do not allow catastrophes so I can teach my children lessons in life. If I did, I would be regarded as an unsafe parent and even placed under arrest as a child abuser. Our loving heavenly Father is a perfect parent. He never allows calamity or injury just to teach us lessons in life. God is a good Father of light, not darkness. He sent Jesus to give us life in abundance.

> *Every good gift and every perfect gift is from above, and comes down from the Father of lights, with whom there is no variation or shadow of turning.*

> James 1:17

> *The thief comes only in order to steal and kill and destroy. I came that they may have and enjoy life, and have it in abundance (to the full, till it overflows).*

> John 10:10, AMPC

God's Garden of Eden

God displayed His will for humanity in the Garden of Eden by creating everything good. "Then God saw everything that He had made, and indeed it was very good" (Genesis 1:31). God affirms His creation as "good" six times in Genesis (Genesis 1:10, 12, 18, 21, 25, 31). The Garden of Eden was created without the presence of evil or calamity. God's commandment to Adam demonstrated His divine will that mankind never have knowledge of evil. Mankind was to only experience good from the tree of life and never experience evil or calamity (Genesis 2:9, 17).

It was God's plan since the Garden of Eden for humanity to live without disruption or disharmony. God intended for you to

15

live free from pain, sorrow, and fear. Adam's sin delivered to humanity everything God did not want people to experience including death, disasters, and destruction. It was never the will of God for mankind to have knowledge of anything bad or corrupt. Sin introduced to humanity the knowledge of everything that is evil and destructive.

Should Not Perish

I'm sure you have heard of horrifying things happening to innocent children. These are not acts of God but demonic acts of evil. You may have heard someone refer to an awful tragedy as "an act of God." They may have suggested that the tragedy was allowed by God because He works in mysterious ways beyond our understanding. This well-meaning individual may have even used scriptures taken out of context to support their explanation as to why God allowed the tragedy to happen. It has been taught erroneously that these heartbreaks are a part of God's mysterious sovereignty that will eventually work out for your good.

To say that it is the will of Father God for anyone to be destroyed contradicts the words of Jesus Christ. In Matthew 18:14, Jesus states, "Even so it is not the will of your Father who is in heaven that one of these little ones should perish." Father God sent Jesus to provide for mankind His salvation, healing, provision, and protection.

> *For God so loved the world that He gave His only begotten Son, that whoever believes in Him should not perish but have everlasting life.*

John 3:16

God would never permit anyone to steal from, kill, or destroy His children; He is the giver of life, not the taker of life (John 10:10). All death, destruction, devastation, disaster, and disease are demonic and vehemently against the will of the Father. Jesus gave us the new covenant perspective of the Father's character and nature when He said He is the good shepherd who will always protect His sheep.

New Covenant Perspective

As a born-again believer, you are under the new covenant in the blood of Christ (Matthew 26:28). The new covenant perspective of the nature and character of God was revealed by Jesus Christ.

No one has seen God at any time. The only begotten Son, who is in the bosom of the Father, He has declared Him.

John 1:18

Jesus Christ gives us the true and complete picture of Father God. When the disciples saw Jesus, they saw Father God.

Jesus said to him, "I am the way, the truth, and the life. No one comes to the Father except through Me. If you had known Me, you would have known My Father also; and from now on you know Him and have seen Him."

Philip said to Him, "Lord, show us the Father, and it is sufficient for us."

Jesus said to him, "Have I been with you so long, and yet you have not known Me, Philip? He who has seen Me has seen the Father."

John 14:6-9

Our perspective of God's nature and character is not to be based on someone's teaching, a denomination, tradition, or doctrines of men. The only One who shows us the true and complete portrait of Father God is Jesus Christ and Him alone. Jesus said that no one has seen Father God, that He is the one who has declared Him (John 1:18). No one comes to the Father except through Jesus

17

Christ (John 14:6). When you see the Bible through Jesus Christ and Him alone, then you get the true perspective of Father God.

Father God sent Jesus to bring us good gifts: "If you then, being evil, know how to give good gifts to your children, how much more will your Father who is in heaven give good things to those who ask Him" (Matthew 7:11). There is not one example in the four gospels of Jesus bringing harm or evil to anyone based on the Father's sovereignty. God sent Jesus to do His sovereign will on earth, to bring His goodness, peace, healing, protection, and salvation.

When Jesus taught His disciples on prayer, He said to pray to the Father, "Your will be done on earth as it is in heaven" (Luke 11:2). The Father's will for humanity is the same as His will for the inhabitants of Heaven. He desires that no one hurt, that all is well, that everyone enjoy a life of goodness and happiness.

No Dissension in the Godhead

I was raised in Ohio around farmers. My dad is a farmer. My uncle is a farmer. Grandpa was a farmer. Great Grandpa was a farmer. They all talk, think, and act like farmers because they are farmers. When my uncle needs help on his farm, my dad stops what he is doing, jumps in the truck and helps him out. When a neighbor has an emergency that requires outside help, he can call a nearby farmer and they will work together. Why? They are all farmers. They all have a common goal - to raise a harvest crop. They are not trying to compete with each other or cause the other one to go bankrupt. They all have the same mindset and desire. They enjoy farming and want each other to prosper and be successful in their business. The Godhead works in similar fashion.

Father God does not compete against Jesus Christ, and Jesus Christ never competes against Father God. The Holy Spirit never decides to do His own thing. The Godhead works together doing the same business. They are one in unity with the same objective - to do good for mankind. Acts 10:38 states, "How God anointed

Jesus of Nazareth with the Holy Spirit and with power, who went about **doing good** and healing all who were oppressed by the devil, for God was with Him" (emphasis mine). The Godhead was all involved when Jesus went about doing good and healing all. Father God was with Jesus every time He did good and the Holy Spirit empowered Him.

"Doing Good" Business

During the earthly ministry of Jesus, He did the will of His Father, which was to do good and not evil. When Jesus healed them all, He was doing the Father's will. Jesus knew at an early age that He was sent only to do the will of His Father. At age twelve, Jesus asked His earthly parents, "Why do you seek Me? Did you not know that I must be about My Father's business?" (Luke 2:49). God the Father is in the *"Doing Good" Business*! Jesus the Son of God is in the *"Doing Good" Business*! And the Holy Spirit is in the *"Doing Good" Business*! There is no division or confusion in the Godhead. God is good all the time.

If you need anything good, look to God who is in the *"Doing Good" Business*. If you need healing for your body, look to God who is in the *"Healing All" Business*. If you need protection, look to God who is in the *"Divine Protection" Business*. God can be trusted. He will keep you from all harm and danger.

> *The LORD shall preserve you from all evil; He shall preserve your soul. The LORD shall preserve your going out and your coming in from this time forth, and even forevermore.*

> Psalm 121:7-8

The Gospel of Peace

The more you hear and understand God's promises of divine protection, the more faith will grow inside your heart. Romans 10:15 states, "As it is written: 'How beautiful are the feet of those who preach the gospel of peace, who bring glad tidings of good things!'"

The Hebrew word for "peace" is *shalom*, which is defined by Strong's Exhaustive Concordance as: "safety, welfare, health, prosperity, peace, rest, all is well, wholeness." The meaning of shalom is also understood to include unharmed and unhurt.[1] The gospel of peace includes welfare, safety, and divine protection. When you were born again into the family of God, you and your entire family were given a blood covenant right of divine peace and protection. It is vital for you to know and believe what God's Word declares for your everyday safety. Your heavenly Father desires for you to live in tranquility with an assurance that no evil can come near you. Listening to the good news of the gospel of peace will cause faith to rise up and fear to dissipate. "But whoever listens to me will dwell safely, and will be secure, without fear of evil" (Proverbs 1:33).

The gospel of peace will make you a new person on the inside. You will become bold and fearless. You will not tolerate being bullied by fear, worry, or anxiety. When you believe and receive the gospel of peace, it is a new day for you and your family. It is a new day of peace! It is a new day of dominion! It is a new day of living on earth in the secret place of protection.

CHAPTER 2

1ST KEY: YOU MUST DWELL IN THE SECRET PLACE

Did you ever watch Cecil B. DeMille's movie, *The Ten Commandments*? I remember when I saw it for the first time, I really enjoyed watching Charlton Heston play the role of Moses. He depicted Moses as a man of courage who was passionate about delivering the children of Israel. However, there was one part of the movie that really puzzled me. It was the scene of Passover night where Moses is in the house of his brother and sister singing verses from Psalm 91. I thought to myself, *Moses couldn't have sung Psalm 91; it was written by King David over six hundred years later!* I found out later why it made sense for Moses to be singing Psalm 91 in that scene. Commentators and rabbis believe that Psalm 91 was authored by Moses.[2]

Song of Moses

In Deuteronomy 32, we find the "Song of Moses;" a poetic song that was to be learned and confessed by the children of Israel.

In this song, Moses likened the way the Lord encircled Jacob to the way an eagle spreads out his wings: "He encircled him, He instructed him, He kept him as the apple of His eye. As an eagle stirs up its nest, hovers over its young, spreading out its wings, taking them up, carrying them on its wings" (Deuteronomy 32:10-11).

In Deuteronomy 33, the final words of Moses are declared over each of the tribes of Israel. Moses blessed the tribe of Benjamin with divine protection: "Of Benjamin he said: 'The beloved of the LORD shall dwell in safety by Him, who shelters him all the day long; and he shall dwell between His shoulders'" (Deuteronomy 33:12). Moses spoke of the tribe of Asher as leaning underneath the everlasting arms for a place of refuge: "The eternal God is your refuge, and underneath are the everlasting arms…Then Israel shall dwell in safety" (Deuteronomy 33:27-28). The way to know we are safe and secure from all danger is by dwelling underneath the everlasting arms of the Lord.

A Prayer of Moses the Man of God

The fourth book of Psalms begins with the prayer of Moses in Psalm 90. That psalm begins, "Lord, You have been our dwelling place in all generations" (Psalm 90:1). Psalm 91 begins, "He who dwells in the secret place of the Most High shall abide under the shadow of the Almighty" (Psalm 91:1). Both of these verses describe the Lord as being a dwelling place of refuge. When your trust is in the Lord's protection, He becomes a dwelling place of refuge for you and your entire family.

In Psalm 90:1, the Hebrew word translated "dwelling place" is *mawohn*, which means "dwelling, abode, a retreat, asylum, habitation." [3] In Psalm 91:1, the Hebrew word translated "dwells" is *yashab*, which means "to sit down, to remain, to inhabit, tarry." [4] Both Psalm 90:1 and Psalm 91:1 refer to the *Shechinah* presence of the Lord as a dwelling place of refuge.

Psalm 91 mentions eight keys that will position you in the secret place of supernatural protection. The first key is this: You must dwell in the secret place.

He who dwells in the secret place of the Most High shall abide under the shadow of the Almighty.

Psalm 91:1

Remember, the Hebrew word translated "dwells" in this verse means to sit down, to remain, to inhabit, to tarry. The idea of dwelling and abiding is to remain and continue as a lifestyle. If you are going to dwell in the secret place, then you must remain. You do not run to the secret place when you have an emergency. You dwell, live, remain there. You have the truth of God's Word richly abiding in your heart. His Word is governing your life. You practice His presence on a daily basis. You meditate on His Word day and night. You are in constant communion with the Lord. You listen to His voice and walk in the light of His Word. His presence is your permanent dwelling place. You wake up in His presence and continue in communion with Him throughout the day and night. This starts with a decision to pursue intimacy with the Lord.

The Secret Place

So where is the secret place? The secret place is found when you receive Jesus as your Lord and Savior. The Apostle Paul called the revealing of our redemption "the mystery which has been hidden from ages and from generations, but now has been revealed to His saints" (Colossians 1:26). Had the devil understood the mystery of our redemption, he would have never crucified the Lord.

But we speak the wisdom of God in a mystery, the hidden wisdom which God ordained before the ages for our glory,

23

which none of the rulers of this age knew; for had they known, they would not have crucified the Lord of glory.

1 Corinthians 2:7-8

In other words, when Satan crucified the Lord of glory, he actually planted Him in the ground as a seed. The death, burial, and resurrection of Jesus Christ are what make it possible for us to dwell in the secret place of God Most High.

Did you know that Christ lives in you? John tells us, "You are of God, little children, and have overcome them, because He who is in you is greater than he who is in the world" (1 John 4:4). Even if you received Jesus Christ just a few seconds ago, you are in blood covenant with Father God. Christ, the hope of glory, lives inside your recreated spirit (Colossians 1:27).

When Noah and his family went inside the ark covered in pitch, they were all safe in the hidden place of the ark (Genesis 6:14). When baby Moses was placed inside the floating ark covered in pitch, he was safe in the hidden place of the ark (Hebrews 11:23). When you received Jesus as your Savior, He placed you inside Himself and He came on the inside of you so that you are safely hidden in Christ: "Whoever confesses that Jesus is the Son of God, God abides in him, and he in God" (1 John 4:15).

Choosing to Abide Under His Shadow

Abiding under the shadow of the Almighty is a choice you make. You choose to be in communion with the Lord; you make living in the presence of the Lord your lifestyle. Psalm 91:1 says, "He who dwells in the secret place of the Most High shall abide…". The Hebrew word for "abide" used in verse one is *leen*, which means "to abide, to continue to dwell, remain, to tarry all day and night." [5] When you abide, you sit down and enjoy receiving from Jesus as you feed on His love and His Word.

24

In Luke 10, we see Martha busy and distracted with much serving while her sister Mary sits at the feet of Jesus receiving His Word (Luke 10:39-40). When Martha complains about Mary's failure to help her, Jesus tells Martha that one thing is needed and Mary has chosen it: "And Jesus answered and said to her, 'Martha, Martha, you are worried and troubled about many things. But one thing is needed, and Mary has chosen that good part, which will not be taken away from her'" (Luke 10:41-42).

When you choose to rest at Jesus' feet and make the Word of God your place of habitation, you are choosing to dwell in the secret place. When you fellowship with the Father, you shut out all distractions and center on the Lord who is found in the secret place.

> *But you, when you pray, go into your room, and when you have shut your door, pray to your Father who is in the secret place; and your Father who sees in secret will reward you openly.*

> Matthew 6:6

You may be asking, "How can I abide in His presence and meditate on scriptures all day and night? What am I supposed to do? Read the Bible everywhere I go? Have it tucked under my arm when I go to bed at night?" There are different ways you can practice the presence of God and meditate in His Word other than by going to church or reading your Bible. You can be driving to work listening to good messages in your car. Rather than listening to the news while stuck in traffic, you can rest at the feet of Jesus and listen to the "good news" of God's Word. The key is to always be prepared. If you know you'll be in the waiting room at the doctor's office for a while, bring your Bible and read passages that build your faith. Have God's Word already loaded on your phone or tablet. Also, listening to anointed music is a way to create an atmosphere of praise and worship.

You can receive fresh manna from heaven by listening to anointed music as you type on the computer at work. Everyone else may be like Martha – busy, distracted, anxious and worried - but you have chosen the better thing. You are like Mary sitting at the feet of Jesus. You are dwelling in the secret place. Can you imagine being at the grocery store where everyone is complaining about the slow cashier, but you are meditating on God's promises with a glowing smile on your face? The cashier might think you are happy about the price of milk!

I've heard people say to my wife, "You have such a joyful countenance." They are observing a person who dwells in the secret place of the Lord. When you practice God's presence and meditate on His Word everywhere you go, you will abide under the shadow of the Almighty.

Meditate Day and Night

This Book of the Law shall not depart from your mouth, but you shall meditate in it day and night, that you may observe to do according to all that is written in it. For then you will make your way prosperous, and then you will have good success. Have I not commanded you? Be strong and of good courage; do not be afraid, nor be dismayed, for the LORD *your God is with you wherever you go.*

Joshua 1:8-9

If you are going to abide under the shadow of the Almighty, you must learn how to meditate in God's Word both day and night. Your mouth must agree with God's Word, and the only way that will happen is if you meditate on His Word day and night. If your mind is not renewed to God's Word, you will not be strong in faith and will speak wrong words. You will be afraid and dismayed, not realizing that the Lord your God is with you whenever and wherever you go.

The Hebrew word for "meditate" is *hagah*, meaning to reflect, to mutter, to contemplate something as one repeats the words.[6] One understanding of hagah is where the Jewish tradition in prayer called "davening" comes from. You may have seen video of men at the Western Wall in Jerusalem rocking back and forth as they recite texts from the Torah. That is davening. When you meditate, contemplate, and speak God's Word to yourself during the day, it will become nourishment to your recreated spirit during the night.

> *My son, give attention to my words; incline your ear to my sayings. Do not let them depart from your eyes; keep them in the midst of your heart; for they are life to those who find them, and health to all their flesh. Keep your heart with all diligence, for out of it spring the issues of life. Put away from you a deceitful mouth, and put perverse lips far from you.*
>
> Proverbs 4:20-24

The way to get God's Word in your heart is by keeping it in your ears and in front of your eyes and coming out of your mouth. When you meditate in God's Word day and night, it will become alive inside of you. A heart full of deception will produce a "deceitful mouth." A heart full of truth will produce a "fruitful mouth." Your mouth maintains the hedge around you and your family. When you guard your mouth, you preserve your life. When you open wide your mouth, you invite destruction.

> *A man shall eat well by the fruit of his mouth...he who guards his mouth preserves his life, but he who opens wide his lips shall have destruction.*
>
> Proverbs 13:2-3

Abiding in the secret place is not just something you do in times of trouble. When you practice the presence of the Lord and meditate in His Word day and night, abiding in the secret place becomes a lifestyle. Your delight and desire for intimacy and fellowship with the Father will cause you to be firmly planted underneath His shadow.

But his delight and desire are in the law of the Lord, and on His law (the precepts, the instructions, the teachings of God) he habitually meditates (ponders and studies) by day and by night. And he shall be like a tree firmly planted [and tended] by the streams of water, ready to bring forth its fruit in its season; its leaf also shall not fade or wither; and everything he does shall prosper [and come to maturity].

Psalm 1:2-3, AMPC

Start today practicing the presence of the Lord. Delight yourself in His Word. Keep your mind focused on Jesus. Throughout the day, thank Him for His goodness, His mercy, and His unfailing love. When you meditate on Him during the day, you'll find yourself meditating in His Word during the night.

CHAPTER 3

2ND KEY: YOU MUST SAY WITH YOUR MOUTH

He who dwells in the secret place of the Most High shall abide under the shadow of the Almighty. I will say of the LORD, "He is my refuge and my fortress; my God, in Him I will trust."

Psalm 91:1-2

Psalm 91 gives us the second key to living a life of supernatural protection, and that is we must say out loud what we believe in our hearts - that the Lord is our dwelling place of refuge: "I will say of the LORD, 'He is my refuge and my fortress; my God, in Him I will trust'" (Psalm 91:2).

The Hebrew word for "refuge" used in this verse is *machceh*, which means, "a place of safety or protection from enemies."[7] The Hebrew word for "shadow" is *tsel*, which means "a defense shade."[8] To get a mental picture of this idea of a defense shade, picture a giant standing behind you and the shade from their shadow covers you. The shadow of the Almighty is your defense shade. Can you picture God as our secret place of protection? He is our Father, the most powerful, the strongest of any other, the maker of the universe, creator of life, and He stands over us as we dwell safely in His shade of protection. When we see ourselves dwelling safely underneath the shadow of the Most High, the Almighty, the great I AM, the omnipotent creator of life and maker of the universe, then we will fearlessly declare, "He is our refuge and our fortress; in Him we will trust!"

Faith Is Released in Words

You may have heard someone say, "Let us keep our brother in our thoughts and prayers." Keeping a person in your thoughts is good, but it is not enough. The hedge of divine protection is enforced by words that are spoken from the mouth. It is when you believe in your heart and release God's Word from your mouth that faith becomes effective.

When faith in your heart is released by words from your mouth, then the power of God is manifested. These words come directly from your recreated spirit, releasing by faith the power of God to bring the supernatural into the natural. When you declare out of your mouth, "The Lord is my refuge. He is my fortress. In Him I put my trust," the blood covenant of protection is released into the realm of the natural. Angels of God are put on alert when you speak God's Word in faith.

> *Bless the LORD, you His angels, who excel in strength, who do His word, heeding the voice of His word.*

> Psalm 103:20

You must give voice to God's Word. The angel of the Lord responded to Daniel's spoken prayer saying, "I have come because of your words" (Daniel 10:12). When you declare by faith that the Lord is your refuge and fortress, angels will heed to the voice of God's Word. Angels must hear the voice of God's Word

30

coming out of your mouth if they are to administer that Word. Remember, Psalm 103:20 does not say angels heed to God's *written* Word but to God's *spoken* Word.

Angels have been given the task of keeping the heirs of salvation safe in all their ways: "Are they not all ministering spirits sent forth to minister for those who will inherit salvation" (Hebrews 1:14). Note that the angels are sent forth to minister for us, which is why it is vital for you to believe and speak in agreement with the truth of God's Word. If you say things like, "Well, I'll see you tomorrow…if the Lord's willing," you are questioning the truth of God's Word. The Bible clearly promises us longevity, which would certainly include tomorrow: "With long life I will satisfy him and show him My salvation" (Psalm 91:16). If you say, "Lord, be with us and please don't ever leave us," you are questioning God's promise to never leave you or forsake you (Hebrews 13:5). You are to declare that the Lord will never leave and that He is watching over you as you travel because Scripture tells us, "I will set him on high, because he knows and understands My name [has a personal knowledge of My mercy, love, and kindness – trusts and relies on Me, knowing I will never forsake him, no, never]" (Psalm 91:14, AMPC).

So what should you say? Agree with God's Word in all things. The angels cannot heed to the voice of doubt and unbelief. The angels only respond according to the truth of God's Word. When you agree with God's Word, it enforces the angels to keep you in all your ways (Psalm 91:11).

The Power of the Tongue

When your heart is filled with God's Word and that Word is spoken from your lips, the power of life is released.

A man's stomach shall be satisfied from the fruit of his mouth; from the produce of his lips he shall be filled.

Death and life are in the power of the tongue, and those who love it will eat its fruit.

Proverbs 18:20-21

The power of both life and death is released from your heart and comes out of your mouth in words. When you speak God's promises of divine protection, supernatural power for your safety is released. The angels are enforced. The divine hedge is impenetrable. The shelter of the secret place is indestructible. When you declare with your voice the Lord's salvation, the power of His Christ is released.

Then I heard a loud voice saying in heaven, "Now salvation, and strength, and the kingdom of our God, and the power of His Christ have come, for the accuser of our brethren, who accused them before our God day and night, has been cast down. And they overcame him by the blood of the Lamb and by the word of their testimony."

Revelation 12:10-11

Chaos is rampant throughout the earth because the devil knows his time is short. He knows we are living in the last days. The devil, who is the accuser of the brethren, will always try to deceive you so you will not speak your faith in the blood of Jesus. He will accuse you day and night, reminding you of your past mistakes and failures. He does not want you to believe and declare that you are the righteousness of God in Christ Jesus by faith in the blood. It is vital that you daily and frequently declare your testimony that you are cleansed and justified by the precious blood of the Lamb.

Much more then, having now been justified by His blood, we shall be saved from wrath through Him.

Romans 5:9

The devil will try to convince you that the words of your mouth are irrelevant and unimportant. He does not want you to believe that you can release the power of Christ with your words. The way you overcome the devil is by faith in the blood of Jesus and by declaring His Word with your mouth, "I will say of the LORD, He is my refuge and my fortress; my God, in Him I will trust" (Psalm 91:2). When you believe in the blood of Jesus and declare His divine protection over you, there is nothing the enemy can do to harm you. You are cleansed by the blood. You are washed by the blood. You are protected by the blood. But you must do more than believe it; you must declare it: "And since we have the same spirit of faith, according to what is written, 'I believed and therefore I spoke,' we also believe and therefore speak" (2 Corinthians 4:13).

Declare this right now over you and your entire family:

> *"I cover myself and my entire family with the precious blood of Jesus and declare that we dwell in the secret place of the Most High. We abide under the shadow of the Almighty. I will say of the Lord, He is our refuge and our fortress; He is our God, and in Him we will trust."*

> -Psalm 91:1-2, paraphrased

Perilous Pestilence

> *Surely He shall deliver you from the snare of the fowler and from the perilous pestilence. He shall cover you with His feathers, and under His wings you shall take refuge; His truth shall be your shield and buckler.*

> Psalm 91:3-4

We are told that we will face perilous times in the last days: "But know this, that in the last days perilous times will come" (2 Timothy 3:1). Luke 21:11 gives us some insight into what those perilous times will look like: "There will be mighty and violent earthquakes, and in various places famines and pestilences (plagues: malignant and contagious or infectious epidemic diseases which are deadly and devastating); and there will be sights of terror and great signs from heaven" (AMPC). We consistently hear of new viruses and diseases that are plaguing our world. But we have a blood covenant of protection that keeps us safe from all plagues and diseases. We can boldly declare, "Surely He shall deliver us from the snare of the fowler and from the perilous pestilence" (Psalm 91:3). Not "We sure hope so," or "If the Lord is willing," but "Surely."

We should not fear the perilous pestilence. We need not be afraid of catching anything deadly or dangerous when we are dwelling in the secret place. Though there may be severe plagues that are harmful and even contagious, they will not come near you. You are protected from every disease and epidemic when you are hidden in the secret place.

Set Apart in the Ark

No contagion or disease in the world today or tomorrow can penetrate the fortress of the Lord. In the case of Noah, the danger outside could not penetrate the ark covered with pitch. God himself instructed Noah how to build the ark, telling him to cover it with pitch. the same Hebrew word for "cover" here - kahfar - is often translated "atonement," as its definition includes to cover over, atone, or to signify as a place of shelter. God established His blood covenant of protection with Noah and his family, so as long as they stayed in the ark, no harm came to them (Genesis 6:18).

In much the same way, Moses and the Israelites were set apart from the plagues that came upon Egypt in Exodus chapters 7-11 because they made the Lord their refuge and fortress.

As long as we stay inside the ark of the Lord's protection, we are sheltered from all deadly and devastating diseases and epidemics that are plaguing our world.

Cover You with His Wings

Psalm 91:4 paints a beautiful word picture of the protection God provides His children: "He shall cover you with His feathers, and under His wings you shall take refuge; His truth shall be your shield and buckler." Have you ever seen a mother hen protecting her little chicks? Growing up around farmers, I would often see Dad or Grandpa feeding the little chicks. When the mother hen saw that someone was coming too close, she would gather her little chicks under her protective wings because she is momma!

Jesus expressed His desire to keep Jerusalem underneath His protective wings: "O Jerusalem, Jerusalem, the one who kills the prophets and stones those who are sent to her! How often I wanted to gather your children together, as a hen gathers her chicks under her wings, but you were not willing! See! Your house is left to you desolate" (Matthew 23:37-38). The children of God could have been hiding under the shadow of the Lord, but they refused to receive His protection. They were not willing to gather together underneath His wings.

When you rush to work, hurriedly drop your children at school, run errands, and never bother to pray for the Lord's protection, you are doing the same thing as the inhabitants of Jerusalem. You are showing an unwillingness to gather underneath the Lord's wings of protection. He intently desires for you and your entire family to rest safely underneath His wings of protection. If you remain unwilling to gather underneath His protection, you will find your house left desolate. There is NOTHING more important for you to do for the sake of you and your family than to gather together safely underneath the Lord's protection - nothing happening at work, nothing with the PTA, nothing at soccer practice, nothing at ballet - absolutely nothing!

My wife recently told me she had been chased away by a mockingbird. She was taking her walk when suddenly a mockingbird came screeching, diving at her head. I did some research and discovered that when a mockingbird feels he or his young are in danger, he will screech at the perceived danger and even graze at the top of a person's head. Think about how big our God is and how gigantic His wings of glory must be. When the devil is trying to threaten you, don't be afraid. The giant wings of God's presence will come to your rescue.

Regardless of the threat, our Lord promises to cover us with His protective wings. Just as the wings of the cherubs stretched over the Ark of the covenant (Exodus 25:10-22), so the Lord covers us with His mercy and protection. As long as we put our trust in Him, we know that we are safely hidden inside His shelter. The truth of God's Word is what shields us all around, encompassing us closely on all sides (Psalm 91:4).

Healing in His Wings

When you are safely dwelling under the wings of the Lord's protection there is no pestilence or sickness present – only healing.

> *But to you who fear My name the Sun of Righteousness shall arise with healing in His wings; and you shall go out and grow fat like stall-fed calves.*

Malachi 4:2

The *Complete Jewish Bible* translation adds additional nuance to this verse, "…you will break out leaping, like calves released from the stall." As you feed on God's Word and bask in His presence, you become like a healthy fed calf. You become strong and healthy, leaping for joy. Remember that the joy of the Lord is your strength (Nehemiah 8:10) and in His presence is fullness of joy: "You will show me the path of life; in Your presence is fullness of joy; at Your right hand are pleasures forevermore" (Psalm 16:11).

You are able to live in safety under the wings of the Most High because you have been made righteous by faith in Christ Jesus (Romans 10:10). The Sun of Righteousness has made us sons of His righteousness.

Teach Your Mouth

The heart of the wise teaches his mouth, and adds learning to his lips. Pleasant words are like a honeycomb, sweetness to the soul and health to the bones. There is a way that seems right to a man, but its end is the way of death.

Proverbs 16:23-25

It is not natural that you would speak the Word of God. The way you teach your mouth to speak God's Word is by adding the Word to your heart. When you have God's Word in your heart in abundance, your mouth will overflow with it. As the scripture says, "Out of the abundance of the heart his mouth speaks" (Luke 6:45).

When the doctor informed me that I had a cancer, I meditated on healing scriptures day and night and then confessed those scriptures:

I shall not die, but live, and declare the works of the LORD.

Psalm 118:17

Surely our diseases he did bear, and our pains he carried; whereas we did esteem him stricken, smitten of God, and afflicted. But he was wounded because of our transgressions, he was crushed because of our iniquities: the chastisement of our welfare was upon him, and with his stripes we were healed.

Isaiah 53:4-5, THS

For assuredly, I say to you, whoever says to this mountain, "Be removed and be cast into the sea," and does not doubt in his heart, but believes that those things he says will be done, he will have whatever he says.

Mark 11:23

I would not let those scriptures and other healing promises out of my sight. I said them when I woke up, said them when I was eating breakfast, and said them while I exercised. I even quoted those scriptures while taking a shower! I kept God's Word with me wherever I went. I had the scriptures on index cards, on my cell phone, on my bathroom mirror, and in my wallet. When I waited for hours in the doctor's office, I meditated on the healing scriptures. While others waiting for treatment were watching *The Price is Right*, I figured I had better things to do than watch someone choose door number three. I choose Jesus who is "The Door," the One who paid the price to make it right! I kept God's Word in my mouth by meditating in it day and night.

> *Whoever guards his mouth and tongue keeps his soul from troubles.*

> Proverbs 21:23

I kept a guard over my mouth all the time. I put a watch over my tongue and kept my soul out of trouble. Praise God, I am and will continue to be cancer free!

Keeping God's Word daily in your mouth, in your ears, and in front of your eyes will cause faith to increase in your heart. When you teach your mouth to agree with God's Word, you will receive healing in your body and deliverance from destruction. "He sent His word and healed them, and delivered them from their destructions" (Psalm 107:20).

3ᴿᴰ KEY: YOU SHALL
NOT BE AFRAID

*You shall not be afraid of the terror by night, nor of the
arrow that flies by day, nor of the pestilence that walks in
darkness, nor of the destruction that lays waste at noonday.
A thousand may fall at your side, and ten thousand at your
right hand; but it shall not come near you. Only with your
eyes shall you look, and see the reward of the wicked.*

Psalm 91:5-8

The third key to divine protection is found in Psalm 91,
verse 5: "You shall not be afraid."

The world has assigned all kinds of psychological names to
different types of fears. There seems to be a phobia for anything
and everything.

• *Hydrophobia:* fear of water

- *Ancraophobia:* fear of wind
- *Hypnophobia:* fear of falling asleep
- *Uranophobia:* fear of heaven
- *Papaphobia:* the fear of the Pope
- *Xanthophobia:* the fear of the color yellow
- *Turophobia:* the fear of cheese
- *Nopophobia:* the fear of being without mobile phone coverage (no joke!) [9]

All of these phobias come from the spirit of fear. It is not God's will for you to fear anyone or anything. That is why the Lord commanded His people time and again not to fear (Luke 1:13, Daniel 10:12, Isaiah 41:10 – just to name a few). God has given you His power, His love, and His mind so you may be delivered from all fears. "For God has not given us a spirit of fear, but of power and of love and of a sound mind" (2 Timothy 1:7).

In his book *The Power of the Blood*, H.A. Maxwell Whyte shares how he and his family lived fearlessly in England during World War II.

> The effectiveness of the covering by the blood of Jesus was made very real to Mrs. Whyte and me during World War II when we were living in England. We often experienced dangerous air raids, during which buzz bombs were flying everywhere. But we were able to lie down with our children and sleep through much of the peril. The protection afforded by the blood of Jesus was so real that it seemed as if we were sleeping in a strong shelter. In fact, we used to speak of the blood as the best air-raid shelter in the world. However, we never took this shelter for granted. Instead, every night before we went to sleep, we would cover ourselves, our home, and our children with the blood of Jesus. One night thirteen bombs landed within a three-quarter-mile radius of our home. And they were big

blockbusters. Yet aside from some minor damage to the house, we were all kept safe.[10]

H.A. Maxwell and his wife made the Lord their place of shelter and refuge during perilous times by faith in His blood covenant of protection. They daily spoke over themselves, their children, and their home that they were under the Lord's covering of protection. Just as it did for the Maxwells, dwelling in the secret place will enable you to lie down in peace (Psalm 4:8). Fear cannot be present when you are trusting in the Lord's protection.

In ancient times, a country would throw a spear or shoot an arrow into the country they intended to invade. This was to notify that country that they had thirty days to negotiate a peaceable settlement before they were attacked. If no settlement was reached in that timeframe, war would begin. This method of warning of imminent attack was not only used to prompt peace settlements, but it was also used to build fear in the hearts of those about to be attacked.[11]

Terrorists are experts at putting fear into the hearts of their victims. Their primary strategy is to use fear as a weapon. If a terrorist cannot make you afraid, they have failed. The way to rid fear from your heart is to allow God's unconditional love to flush it out.

Unconditional Love Flushes out Fear

God's love for you is unconditional. He does not love you only on your good days. He loves you on your worst day. God loves you regardless of your imperfections and performance. The unconditional love of your heavenly Father frees you from any fear.

> *There is no fear in love; but perfect love casts out fear, because fear involves torment. But he who fears has not been made perfect in love.*

> 1 John 4:18

The Greek word translated "love" in this verse is *agape*, which refers to God's unconditional love. The Father's unconditional love is perfect. When you receive the unconditional love of the Father, it empowers you to live a fearless life. When you believe and declare that His unconditional love surrounds you on every side, it removes all doubts and fears.

Does the protection of the Father leave when you stumble into sin? Can the enemy rush in and take your life? If that were true, then none of us would be alive. The devil would have killed us a long time ago, the moment we sinned. The truth is the blood of Jesus has cleansed us from all unrighteousness (1 John 1:7). The love of the Father does not fade away. His love is unconditional, unchanging, everlasting, and perfect.

In order to live without fear, you must be persuaded that Father God loves you unconditionally. The devil will challenge you with the lie that God's love is conditional. Satan will accuse you, saying you are not worthy of God's love and protection. That is why you must know that divine protection is based upon faith in the blood covenant. You do not deserve divine protection but by faith in Christ's blood, you have received the promise of divine protection.

> *For I am persuaded that neither death nor life, nor angels nor principalities nor powers, nor things present nor things to come, nor height nor depth, nor any other created thing, shall be able to separate us from the love of God which is in Christ Jesus our Lord.*

Romans 8:38-39

The enemy will try to speak lies into your mind like, "You can't depend on God's protection, you sorry, no good sinner. You don't deserve His protection!" The devil will bring thoughts of fear about your teenager getting hurt or killed because of their unworthiness. When you believe this lie, it's called "sin consciousness" and it feeds fear into the heart. Don't tolerate fear!

None of us deserve divine protection. In fact, we don't deserve any of the promises of God. You believe and receive the promise of divine protection based on your faith in the blood covenant. Nothing else. The Father's perfect love for you will cast out the fear of your inadequacy. Perfect love is based on God's unconditional love for you and not on anything you think you have done or have failed to do. You can live unafraid because you believe in God's perfect love for you. Your confidence in the Lord's love and protection empowers you to say, "The LORD is on my side; I will not fear. What can man do to me?" (Psalm 118:6).

Have you ever had the thought, "I hope that something bad doesn't happen to me or to my children"? This is a thought of fear and is not grounded in the Father's love. When you question the Lord's protection, it is because you lack trust in His perfect love for you. You think the Lord has left you alone because you disappointed Him, then that opens the door for fear to come in. Always believe that the Lord is with you and is for you, no matter what you feel or don't feel, no matter what you see or don't see. He is with you and for you so you never have to be afraid.

Psalm 23

One of the most well-known of David's writings is Psalm 23, which speaks of the Lord as a shepherd who protects His sheep from enemies and life-threatening disaster.

> *The LORD is my shepherd; I shall not want. He makes me to lie down in green pastures; He leads me beside the still waters. He restores my soul; He leads me in the paths of righteousness for His name's sake. Yea, though I walk through the valley of the shadow of death, I will fear no evil; for You are with me; Your rod and Your staff, they comfort me. You prepare a table before me in the presence of my enemies; You anoint my head with oil; my cup runs over. Surely goodness and mercy shall follow me all the*

days of my life; and I will dwell in the house of the LORD forever.

In the Amplified Bible, verses 1 and 4 read this way: "The Lord is my Shepherd [to feed, guide, and shield me], I shall not lack...Yes, though I walk through the [deep, sunless] valley of the shadow of death, I will fear or dread no evil, for You are with me; Your rod [to protect] and Your staff [to guide], they comfort me" (Psalm 23:1, 4, AMPC).

Notice the reason David did not fear while walking through the sunless valley was because he knew that the Lord was with him and was a shield around him. Father God is not going to leave you when you face a dark and bleak path. You have to believe that the only thing God has following you is His goodness, grace, and mercy.

> *Goodness and grace will pursue me every day of my life; and I will live in the house of Adonai for years and years to come.*

Psalm 23:6, CJB

I Will Never Leave You

God freely gives us His protection because He is for us and will never forsake us.

> *For He Himself has said, "I will never leave you nor forsake you." So we may boldly say: "The LORD is my helper; I will not fear. What can man do to me?"*

Hebrews 13:5-6

When you know that Father God is on your side, you will boldly say, "My Father will never leave me. He will never forsake me. The Lord is my helper; I will not fear. What can man do to me?"

Have you ever looked to your past with regret? You may be reading this book feeling like the bad things that happened to you in the past were a result of God's judgment. We have all messed up. None of us are perfect. When you look to your past, you need to see it the same way God sees it - washed by the blood of the Lamb.

> *What then shall we say to these things? If God is for us,*
> *who can be against us? He who did not spare His own Son,*
> *but delivered Him up for us all, how shall He not with Him*
> *also freely give us all things?*

> Romans 8:31-32

The only thing you should say to the devil's accusations is "God is for me and not against me!" If the accuser says, "Well the reason that tragedy happened in your past is because God abandoned you," you need to respond, "No devil, you are a liar! Father God is for me and He has never left me nor forsaken me!" Know that the more you say aloud that God is for you and not against you, that He will never leave you nor forsake you, the devil's lying accusations will be drowned in the fountain of Jesus' blood. When your faith is in the blood of Jesus, the devil always loses. God's goodness and mercy have been following you and will continue to follow you all the days of your life (Psalm 23:6).

The Good Shepherd

Jesus referred to Himself as being a good shepherd: "I am the good shepherd. The good shepherd gives His life for the sheep" (John 10:11). The Lord reassured David that He was with him always: "Goodness and grace will pursue me every day of my life" (Psalm 23:6, CJB). David knew the Lord would protect him when he passed through unsafe places. The Lord not only escorts us, but He guards and shields us: "The Lord is my Shepherd [to feed, guide, and shield me], I shall not lack" (Psalm 23:1, AMPC).

The sheep follow the Good Shepherd because they trust in Him. They are not afraid of evil because they know the Good Shepherd will protect them: "I will fear or dread no evil, for You are with me; Your rod [to protect] and Your staff [to guide], they comfort me" (Psalm 23:4, AMPC).

So the next time you hear of a terrorist attack or a catastrophe, don't entertain any thought of fear. Declare with boldness, *"The Lord is my shepherd. I shall not want. He feeds me, He guides me, and He protects me. Even when I walk through the valley of the shadow of death, I will fear no evil for He is with me."*

I Will Lie Down in Peace

What if you hear about a mass shooting in your city? Do you stay up all night, afraid you and your family may be the next targets?

> *You shall not be afraid of the terror by night, nor of the arrow that flies by day, nor of the pestilence that walks in darkness, nor of the destruction that lays waste at noonday. A thousand may fall at your side, and ten thousand at your right hand; but it shall not come near you. Only with your eyes shall you look, and see the reward of the wicked.*

> Psalm 91:5-8

If you are a believer, fear is not a natural response to any situation. Let me say that again because I know this truth is contrary to everything the world will tell you: Fear is not a natural response for a believer. Jesus destroyed the power of death and has released us from the fear of death (Hebrews 2:14-15). We have been delivered from all fear. We do not have to fear. If you are afraid, it is because you have chosen to be afraid. You do not have to fear anything or anyone because you dwell in the secret place of the Lord's protection.

Do you rise up in the middle of the night every time you hear a noise? I remember one time our children were staying away at their grandparents' house. The house was so quiet that night without the kids at home. All of a sudden, we heard a noise and the upstairs light came on. Our kids were not upstairs so we wondered who turned on the light. I immediately jumped out of bed and without hesitation, ran up the stairs. Apparently, the switch had been stuck and got unstuck in the middle of the night. I simply fixed the switch and went back to peaceful sleep. Was I not afraid because I know Jiu-Jitsu? Not at all. I knew that our house was covered by the blood of Jesus and no harm could come near. I had peace knowing that we are dwelling in the hidden place of protection.

Do you let fear steal your sleep? Do you lay awake thinking fearful thoughts? God has given you the promise of sweet sleep. When you meditate on the promises of God's protection, you will lie down in peace and will not be afraid.

> *You would also lie down, and no one would make you afraid; Yes, many would court your favor.*   Job 11:18-19

> *I will both lie down in peace, and sleep; For You alone, O LORD, make me dwell in safety.*   Psalm 4:8

> *Then you will walk safely in your way, and your foot will not stumble. When you lie down, you will not be afraid; Yes, you will lie down and your sleep will be sweet.* Proverbs 3:23-24

> *For they shall feed their flocks and lie down, and no one shall make them afraid.*   Zephaniah 3:13

You are not to be afraid during the day or night. You are to lie down in peace and never be afraid. Every night before I go to sleep, I cover myself and my family with the blood of Jesus and say, *"We shall lie down and not be afraid and our sleep shall be sweet. For the Lord is our refuge and our fortress. He is our God and in Him we will trust."*

Delivered from Fear

When Adam sinned in the Garden of Eden, the first knowledge of evil he experienced was fear. Adam partook from the tree of the knowledge of good and evil, which caused him to die spiritually. The voice of God no longer brought him comfort but produced fear: "So he said, 'I heard Your voice in the garden, and I was afraid'" (Genesis 3:10). Sin caused Adam and all of mankind to fear death.

God the Father sent Jesus to deliver us from the fear of death:

> *Inasmuch then as the children have partaken of flesh and blood, He Himself likewise shared in the same, that through death He might destroy him who had the power of death, that is, the devil, and release those who through fear of death were all their lifetime subject to bondage.*

Hebrews 2:14-15

Before Jesus destroyed death, mankind was in bondage to fear. All fear is based in the fear of death. There is not one person on this planet who enjoys talking about death, unless they are born again. Every person who is not born again is afraid of death, afraid of God's wrath, and afraid to face eternity. It is impossible for a sinner to have peace about death. A person may hide their feelings out of pride and say they are not afraid of dying, but the truth is all mankind is subject under bondage of the fear of death.

When you embrace what Jesus did on the cross and receive His righteousness by faith in His blood, you no longer have to be afraid of death or of God's wrath. You must have your mind renewed according to God's Word and His unconditional love (1 John 4:16). You no longer have to allow fear to torment you because you have been set free by receiving the Spirit of adoption.

For you did not receive the spirit of bondage again to fear, but you received the Spirit of adoption by whom we cry out, "Abba, Father."

Romans 8:15

What happens to you inside when you hear the media reports about death, destruction, terrorism, or plagues? Do such reports cause you to be afraid? You no longer have to fear, because you have received the Spirit of adoption: "For God has not given us a spirit of fear, but of power and of love and of a sound mind" (2 Timothy 1:7). When you embrace Your Father's love, it will keep you in perfect peace regardless of the turmoil around you: "You will keep him in perfect peace, whose mind is stayed on You, because he trusts in You" (Isaiah 26:3). You do not have to tolerate fear.

Facing the Fear of Cancer

When I sat in the doctor's office and heard him say to me, "You have cancer," I had a choice to make. I could either trust in the Lord as my healer, or I could meditate on the doctor's analysis and be full of fear. When the specialist looked at my charts and I heard him say to me, "This does not look good. This is not what I wanted to see. You may have cancer in both your lungs and bones," I had to make a choice. I could choose to believe the lies of the devil when he told me, "Your wife will become a widow and your children will become fatherless," or I could believe in the truth of God's Word. I made the choice to not fear cancer.

You will not be afraid of diseases [or the pestilence] that come [walks; stalks] in the dark or sickness [stings] that strikes [devastates; overpowers] at noon. At your side one thousand people may die [fall], or even ten thousand right beside you [at your right hand], but you will not be hurt [it will not touch you].

Psalm 91:6-7, EXB

I had to resist the fear of cancer that attacked my mind. I could have allowed guilt, condemnation, and shame to creep into my spirit. I could have struggled to figure out why cancer had invaded my body. Was it because I had been eating so much junk food? Was it because I drive on the highway with my windows down and breathe in the toxic air? Did it come from my family's blood line? All those scenarios could be factual, but there is an overriding truth that trumps them all. God's Word is truth and it overrides any other facts. It may be a fact that you have been given a bad report, but the truth of God's Word changes the facts. It was a fact that the servants were serving pitchers of water at the wedding feast, but Jesus, who is the truth, changed the water into wine (John 2:1-10). Truth changed the facts.

It was a fact that a cancerous tumor was in my body, but I chose the truth, which changed the facts. I made the choice not to fear cancer. I chose to believe God's Word. I chose to put my faith in the blood of Jesus and discern the Lord's body. Even though there have been people in my family who died of cancer, I chose to place my trust in my heavenly bloodline. I declared, *"Cancer! You will not kill me! You will not live as a parasite in my body. The blood of Jesus destroys every cancer cell in my body, and by His stripes I am healed. I shall live and not die and will declare the works of the Lord!"*

I chose to believe the truth of God's Word that I shall live and not die, and I will declare the works of the Lord (Psalm 118:17). I refused to accept the facts as truth. That is why I am alive and well today. The truth of God's Word will change the facts when you believe and refuse to fear.

You can decide to not be afraid of anything including tragedy, accidents, terrorism, or plagues. As a child of the Most High, you do not have to fear. When you choose not to fear and instead, feed on God's Word, His love will flush out every ounce of doubt, worry, and anxiety. Let your mind and mouth become so saturated with God's Word, His blood, and His love that no matter what you may be facing right now, fear will no longer torment you.

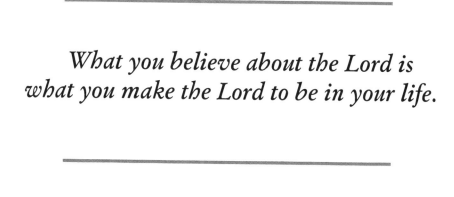

What you believe about the Lord is
what you make the Lord to be in your life.

☙

CHAPTER 5

4ᵀᴴ KEY: YOU HAVE MADE THE LORD YOUR REFUGE

Because you have made the LORD, who is my refuge, even the Most High, your dwelling place, no evil shall befall you, nor shall any plague come near your dwelling.

Psalm 91:9-10

The fourth key to divine protection is found in Psalm 91, verse 9: Make the Lord, the Most High, your refuge and dwelling place. When the Lord is your dwelling place, no evil can come near your dwelling.

Ruth the Friend of God

Since we have been engrafted by faith in the blood of Christ, we have access to take refuge under the wings of the Most High. We see an example of this in the book of Ruth. Naomi was a

Jewish widow whose two sons had married Moabite women (Ruth 1:4). Both of her sons died and left behind their Moabite wives. Under the Law of Moses, God prohibited the Moabites to worship with the Jews, even up to the tenth generation (Deuteronomy 23:3). When Naomi insisted her two Moabite daughters-in-law depart so that they might find new husbands, one of them kissed her goodbye but the other one refused to leave: "Orpah kissed her mother-in-law, but Ruth clung to her" (Ruth 1:14). Orpah (not to be confused with *Oprah*), went back to her people and worshiped the gods of Moab (Ruth 1:15). But Ruth refused to let go of her Jewish mother-in-law and made a covenant with her and with the God of Israel: "For wherever you go, I will go; and wherever you lodge, I will lodge; your people shall be my people, and your God my God" (Ruth 1:16).

Ruth's Moabite name means "friend." When Ruth placed her faith in the God of Israel, she became a friend of God. Even though Ruth was a Moabite, she found grace in God's eyes and received divine favor. This Moabite woman was engrafted with Israel when she came into covenant relationship with the God of her mother-in-law. She ended up marring a wealthy Jewish man named Boaz. Ruth the Moabite was also included in the genealogy of Jesus, as she was the great grandmother of King David (Matthew 1:5). This pagan widow was given the blessing of divine protection.

> *The LORD repay your work, and a full reward be given you by the LORD God of Israel, under whose wings you have come for refuge.*

Ruth 2:12

When you dwell underneath the wings of the Lord God of Israel, you will find your place of refuge. Ruth came under the wings of the Lord's protection and found her place of refuge as a friend of God. Today, Jesus calls you His friend: "You are My friends if you do whatever I command you. No longer do I call you servants, for a servant does not know what his master is doing;

but I have called you friends, for all things that I heard from My Father I have made known to you" (John 15:14-15).

What Do You Say of the Lord?

What are you saying of the Lord when trouble comes your way? Do you say, "Here comes another test from God," or do you say, "He is my refuge and my fortress; my God, in Him I will trust"? What you believe about the Lord is what you make the Lord to be in your life. If you say of the Lord that He allows hardships in your life, then that is who He is to you. If you say of the Lord that He is the reason trouble is around the corner, then that is who He is to you. If you say of the Lord that He is the one who tests and tries you with evil, then that is who He is to you.

You cannot possibly make the Lord your place of refuge and the source of your hardship at the same time. He is either your place of refuge or the source of your problems. He is either the one you trust to do good in your life, or He is the one who cannot be trusted. The Apostle James tells us, "Let no one say when he is tempted, 'I am tempted by God'; for God cannot be tempted by evil, nor does He Himself tempt anyone" (James 1:13). You cannot make the Lord your place of refuge and your place of chaos at the same time. The Lord can only be your place of refuge and safety by right believing.

Is Your Life Like a Roller Coaster?

My family enjoys going to Disney World and Magic Kingdom in Orlando. My kids especially enjoy riding a roller coaster called Space Mountain; Lena and I usually like to stick to the adult rides like It's a Small World. However, many years ago when I was young and single, I decided to ride a roller coaster and learned the hard way not to drink sugary liquids before or after I ride a coaster. I finished guzzling down a jumbo-sized lemonade right before I boarded the bumpy, curvy, swirling, round and round and round and round...roller coaster. I thought the ride was never going to end. No, I was not screaming. In fact, I did everything to keep my mouth shut. I don't think you want to hear the rest of the story! Let's just say I learned my lesson - all the way home!

When I finally got home (after several pit stops on the side of the road), I took a very long and hot shower. I was so glad to be home wearing my nice clean pajamas. I thought to myself, *I will never drink lemonade ever again!* I could have blamed the park for my discomfort, "They should have never allowed me to ride that coaster after I drank their lemonade!" But it was neither the park's fault nor was it the fault of the maker of the lemonade that I got sick. The problem was that I chose to fill my belly with frozen lemonade just before I got on board a roller coaster ride. I was the one to blame.

There are times when God gets the blame for things that simply are not His fault. For example, has your life ever felt like you were on a roller coaster? You or someone else may have said that it was the Lord testing you. You may have believed that He was the One behind the disarray in your life. Let me assure you friend, your Father God was not the perpetrator. He is never the one behind the pandemonium. Your heavenly Father has never been behind any of the chaos that is in this world. God has no dark side; He is never behind anything that is evil.

God Is the Giver of Good Gifts

My wife enjoys opening letters, packages, and especially gifts. I rarely open the mail because she enjoys opening it. Just imagine if I gave my wife an anniversary gift that was in a big box wrapped in sparkly silver paper to commemorate our 20 years together, but when she opened it, out jumped a twelve-foot, sixty-pound boa constrictor! What do you think she would do the next time I gave her a gift? She would probably tell me, "Keep your gift and stay away from my birthday party!"

The only gifts God gives us are good gifts.

Do not be deceived, my beloved brethren. Every good gift and every perfect gift is from above, and comes down from the Father of lights, with whom there is no variation or shadow of turning.

James 1:16-17

Your God is the Father of lights; He is not dark or shady. Your Father God is love and He is good. If what is in your life is not good and perfect, then it is not from the Father of lights. Don't be deceived. Your Father is a place of refuge and protection. He is not the one behind all of the chaos and destruction in the world today. He is your loving Father who wants to give you good gifts to enjoy, not something that would destroy you or your children.

Or what man is there among you who, if his son asks for bread, will give him a stone? Or if he asks for a fish, will he give him a serpent? If you then, being evil, know how to give good gifts to your children, how much more will your Father who is in heaven give good things to those who ask Him!

Matthew 7:9-11

The Lord Bless You and Keep You

In order to believe it is God's desire to protect you, you must understand the gospel. The gospel is "good news." Romans 10:15 states, "As it is written: 'How beautiful are the feet of those who preach the gospel of peace, who bring glad tidings of good things" (Romans 10:15).

When the Lord instructed the priests to bless the children of Israel, He told them to say, "The LORD bless you and keep you…" (Numbers 6:24). The Hebrew word for "keep" in this verse is *shamar*, which means "to hedge about, guard, to protect, attend, to keep, observe, preserve, regard, reserve, save, watch." [12] The blessing the Lord had the priests speak over the children of

Israel began with a reminder that His hedge of protection and safety surrounded them.

The blessing continues, "The LORD make His face shine upon you, and be gracious to you; the LORD lift up His countenance upon you, and give you peace" (Numbers 6:25-26). The Hebrew word shalom is translated "peace" in this verse. Shalom also carries the meaning of health, welfare, safety, and the absence of agitation or discord.[13] When the priest blessed the children of Israel, he released a hedge of blessing to keep them perfectly protected. The blessing of shalom over Israel covered everything they needed for their welfare and safety.

If the message you are hearing is not good news, then it is not the gospel. Hearing and understanding the gospel of peace will produce faith. The gospel includes God's protection for His covenant children who have been born again into the family of God. It is vital for you to know and believe what God's Word declares for your safety. You have a heavenly Father who wants you to live in peace, knowing that no evil shall befall you, nor shall any plague come near your dwelling (Psalm 91:10).

No Evil Shall Befall You

No evil shall befall you, nor shall any plague come near your dwelling.

Psalm 91:10

Jesus appeared to the eleven after His resurrection and commissioned them to go into all the world and preach the good news of the gospel to all nations (Mark 16:15). Jesus did not tell the disciples that as they went to preach the gospel, they would be on their own. Actually, Jesus promised the disciples that they would be protected from all danger.

He gave them power over unclean spirits, to cast them out,
and to heal all kinds of sickness and all kinds of disease.

Mark 16:18

Divine Protection when Traveling

Do you really believe that no evil shall come near your
dwelling place? When you go on a retreat, a business trip, or on a
tour, do you expect that nothing shall by any means hurt you?
When you travel, do you rely on the Lord's protection to keep you
from all harm, sickness, and danger?

Every time I board an airplane, get in a car or taxi or any mode
of transportation, I always cover it with the blood of Jesus. I lay
my hands on the airplane before I board it and declare, "The Lord
is my refuge, my fortress, my God in Him I will trust. I cover this
airplane, the pilot and crew, and all passengers with the blood of
Jesus, in Jesus' name." I sometimes shake the hand of the pilot or
taxi driver and declare over them, "I cover you with the blood of
Jesus!" You might think that would be strange, but many times
they respond with something like, "Thank you. I need the
prayers."

The Apostle Paul trusted in the Lord as his place of refuge
while traveling on his missionary journeys. In one case, Paul and
his companions had been sent to Italy (Acts 26:32-27:1). Luke,
the author of the book of Acts, was present on this ministry
journey and gives a detailed account of his sea voyage to Rome
with Paul and his companions. Luke notes that there were strong
and hazardous winds during this time of the month of October
(Acts 27:9). Sailing on the Mediterranean Sea was considered
dangerous from the end of September through October, and most
would avoid sailing during this time.[14]

Prior to this sea journey to Rome, Paul had endured three
different shipwrecks, including a night and day in the deep: "Three
times I was shipwrecked; a night and a day I have been in the
deep; in journeys often, in perils of waters…in perils in the sea"
(2 Corinthians 11:25-26). He knew from experience that this

journey was dangerous, and he perceived by the Holy Spirit that it would be a disaster: "Men, I perceive that this voyage will end with disaster and much loss, not only of the cargo and ship, but also our lives" (Acts 27:10).

The one in charge of the ship was Julius, a Roman centurion who ignored Paul's warning (Acts 27:1; 11-12). Julius listened to the advice of his captain and continued sailing along the coast of Crete (Acts 27:13). The ship was later met by a violent and tempestuous wind called Euroclydon (Acts 27:14), which means "the wind that stirs up broad waves." [15] The violence of the wind and waves caused the ship to head towards the Syrtis Sands (Acts 27:17), a hazardous area of quicksand off the coast of North Africa west of Cyrene.[16] The storm lasted fourteen days (Acts 27:27), during which the crew threw the cargo overboard to lighten the ship in order to control it better (Acts 27:18-19). Luke notes that the crew of 276 people had gone without food for a long time (Acts 27:21, 37), not because they ran out of food, but because they had given up hope of saving their lives (Acts 27:20). However, Paul declared to them not to lose hope, because an angel appeared to him at night giving him the assurance that everyone on the ship would receive divine protection.

> *And now I urge you to take heart, for there will be no loss of life among you, but only of the ship. For there stood by me this night an angel of the God to whom I belong and whom I serve, saying, "Do not be afraid, Paul; you must be brought before Caesar; and indeed God has granted you all those who sail with you." Therefore take heart, men, for I believe God that it will be just as it was told me.*

Acts 27:22-25

The angel of the Lord appeared to Paul commanding him to not be afraid. Had Paul not believed God but stayed in fear, he would have lost his life along with the lives of all those on the ship. But Paul resisted fear and took heart by believing the words that were told him by the angel. When you travel anywhere, you must believe and declare what you have been told in the Word of God: "Because I have made the Lord, who is my refuge, even the Most

High, my dwelling place, no evil shall befall me! I am covered by the blood of the Lamb" (paraphrase of Psalm 91:9-10).

Divine Protection in Communion

Paul was instructed to land on a certain island and for none of the crew to leave the ship until they arrived (Acts 27:26-31). The sailors attempted to abandon ship to save their own lives, but Paul warned the centurion that if they did not stay on the ship, all of them would die (Acts 27:31). Paul then encouraged the men of the ship by breaking bread and giving thanks to the Lord.

> *And when he had said these things, he took bread and gave thanks to God in the presence of them all; and when he had broken it he began to eat. Then they were all encouraged.*

> Acts 27:35-36

When Paul broke bread, he was acknowledging the Lord's Table. He was discerning the Lord's body and blood (Matthew 26:26-28). No doubt Paul encouraged the men as he gave thanks for the Lord's divine protection, breaking bread in remembrance of His body and His blood of the new covenant. Paul even guaranteed not one hair from their heads would be lost (Acts 27:34).

When you travel, remember to give thanks for the Lord's protection. You can break bread right in your house or in your hotel room and cover it with the blood of Jesus. You don't have to be in church to partake of the Lord's Table. I like to rise up early in the morning and receive communion, recognizing Christ's blood covenant (1 Corinthians 11:23-32). You can daily recognize the Lord's Table as you break bread. Before you sit down to eat your meal, declare the blessing over your food and claim protection from anything poisonous or anything that would cause illness: "… and if they drink anything deadly, it will by no means hurt them" (Mark 16:18).

They Will Take Up Serpents

Paul and his companions recognized the Lord's Table by breaking bread together on the ship and they were all encouraged (Acts 27:35-36). The ship then came near the island of Malta, but the bow and stern were broken up because of the violence of the waves (Acts 27:39-41). The soldiers planned to kill all the prisoners on the ship so that they could not escape, as the escape of the prisoners would cost the soldiers' their lives (Acts 27:42). The centurion prevented the soldiers from killing the prisoners and commanded everyone to abandon ship and go to the island (Acts 27:43-44). Everyone safely made it to the island of Malta, just as the angel told Paul would happen (Acts 27:23-25, 28:1).

The natives of Malta showed kindness to the passengers and crew by making a fire to warm them in the cold weather (Acts 28:1-2). Paul was assisting the natives by laying brushwood on the fire when suddenly, a poisonous viper fastened on his hand (Acts 28:3). The natives saw the viper as a sign that Paul was being judged as a murderer by their pagan goddess: "No doubt this man is a murderer, whom, though he has escaped the sea, yet justice does not allow to live" (Acts 28:4).

The word translated "viper" is the Greek word *echidna*, which refers to a highly venomous snake.[17] The poisonous snake sunk its fangs deep into Paul's flesh and released venom into his hand; the natives knew he would quickly die (Acts 28:3-6). When Paul did not show any signs of being poisoned, they considered him a god: "But he shook off the creature into the fire and suffered no harm. However, they were expecting that he would swell up or suddenly fall down dead. But after they had looked for a long time and saw no harm come to him, they changed their minds and said that he was a god" (Acts 28:5-6).

Luke, a physician, notes that Paul simply shook the venomous serpent off into the fire and never cried out for help. This illustrates how Paul trusted solely in the Lord as his place of refuge and protection. Paul knew Jesus had said that the poisonous snake did not have authority to kill him:

They will take up serpents; and if they drink anything deadly, it will by no means hurt them.

Mark 16:18

Behold, I give you the authority to trample on serpents and scorpions, and over all the power of the enemy, and nothing shall by any means hurt you.

Luke 10:19

Paul and his companions left Malta and safely arrived in Rome where Paul boldly and freely preached for two years (Acts 28:30-31). Consider this example from the life of Paul and the next time you are travelling, make sure you and those with you are dwelling in the secret place of divine protection.

Jumped Like Jordan

The first time Lena and I went to Mexico, we went with a group of other ministers to attend a conference and share the gospel in local churches. When we arrived in Puerto Vallarta, we had the experience of riding in the back seat of a taxi. Before the taxi driver took our luggage, we spoke over him and the car that the angels hedged around us would keep us in all of our ways. When we entered the hotel where we would be staying, we immediately covered it with the blood of Jesus. We also covered all of the ministers who were traveling with us.

Accompanying us on the trip was our nine-month-old son Joshua, who had not even started to crawl. Later in the week, our son was sitting on the bed in the hotel room watching his mother. I had just entered the room when I saw him crawling for the first time…right off the side of the bed! I watched him fall toward the stone floor head first! In a split second, I did a "Michael Jordan leap" from one side of the hotel room to the other. I caught Joshua's heel with one of my hands, when his head was just inches from the floor. I know that in the natural, I can't leap that far. But the angels know how to help you leap as far and as quickly as needed. They can give you NBA leaping abilities and Jedi reflexes.

Anytime you travel, whether to a third world country or just down the street to fill up the tank, you need to always keep safe inside the secret place. It needs to be your daily habit to cover yourself and family with the blood of Jesus and declare the Lord's protection.

CHAPTER 6

ANGELS HAVE CHARGE OVER YOU

For He shall give His angels charge over you, to keep you in all your ways. In their hands they shall bear you up, lest you dash your foot against a stone.

Psalm 91:11-12

Let us look at the first mention of an angel in the Bible. It is found in Genesis 3:24 where a cherubim angel is set to guard the Garden of Eden against any intruder: "So He drove out the man; and He placed cherubim at the east of the garden of Eden, and a flaming sword which turned every way, to guard the way to the tree of life."

Notice how the angel of the Lord protected the Garden of Eden with a flaming sword. The flaming sword turned every way to guard the tree against an intruder. In Psalm 104, the angels are implied to be ministers of fire: "Who makes His angels spirits, His ministers a flame of fire" (Psalm 104:4). When you cover your house, your church, your neighborhood or your city with the blood of Jesus, the angels of fire surround you, protecting you from any intruder. Now, the angels of God are not preventing us *from* coming to the tree of life, but are guarding us as we partake from the tree of life.

The book of Zechariah tells how the Lord would protect Jerusalem with a wall of fire: "'Jerusalem shall be inhabited as towns without walls, because of the multitude of men and livestock in it. For I,' says the LORD, 'will be a wall of fire all around her, and I will be the glory in her midst'" (Zechariah 2:4-5). The Lord protected the city of Jerusalem much like the cherubim guarded the Garden of Eden. Today, the Lord surrounds us with His wall of fire, just as He surrounded Jerusalem.

> *As the mountains surround Jerusalem, so the LORD*
> *surrounds His people from this time forth and forever.*

Psalm 125:2

Angelic Protection Over Jesus

Jesus experienced angelic protection during His time on the earth as the Son of Man. Jesus was afforded protection just after his birth, when His father Joseph was warned by an angel of King Herod's threat: "For Herod will seek the young Child to destroy Him" (Matthew 2:13). When Jesus was tempted in the wilderness, angels ministered to Him, providing for His needs and protecting Him from dangerous, wild beasts (Mark 1:13). Even when He was arrested in the garden of Gethsemane, Jesus knew that He dwelt in the secret place of His Father's protection.

When the religious leaders came to arrest Jesus, He and His disciples were surrounded by a "Roman cohort" comprised of as many as 600 Roman soldiers who were armed with weapons (John 18:2-3, AMP).[18] While those numbers could have seemed overwhelming, Jesus informed Peter and His disciples that He had more than 72,000 angels at His disposal: "Put your sword in its place…do you think that I cannot now pray to My Father, and He will provide Me with more than twelve legions of angels?" (Matthew 26:52-53). To put this in perspective, a full Roman legion was comprised of 6,000 soldiers. That means Jesus had twelve legions of angels ready to defend Him! Jesus reassured His disciples that angelic protection was available, all He had to do was call for help. When you call 911, you may have a couple of police officers come to assist you. When you call on the Lord, His angels will assist you instantaneously.

Angelic Protection in the Early Church

Angelic protection is mentioned throughout the Bible, including in the book of Acts. When the Sadducees heard the message of Jesus and His resurrection from the dead, they were greatly disturbed. Who do you think was behind their hatred of this message? It was Satan, of course. When the number of people being saved was growing through the preaching of the disciples, the devil came to steal the Word that was sown.

> *Being greatly disturbed that they taught the people and preached in Jesus the resurrection from the dead. And they laid hands on them, and put them in custody until the next day, for it was already evening. However, many of those who heard the word believed; and the number of the men came to be about five thousand.*

> Acts 4:2-4

Notice that when the apostles preached and taught in Jesus the resurrection from the dead, the devil got busy trying to kill them. God is never behind the persecution of His preachers. He wills for all of His preachers to live a long life, spreading His good news around the globe. Anytime the gospel is preached, persecution will come from the devil.

The apostles were put into the common prison by the high priest and the sect of the Sadducees for refusing to stop preaching the gospel of Jesus Christ.

> *Then the high priest rose up, and all those who were with him (which is the sect of the Sadducees), and they were filled with indignation, and laid their hands on the apostles and put them in the common prison. But at night an angel of the Lord opened the prison doors and brought them out, and said, "Go, stand in the temple and speak to the people all the words of this life." And when they heard that, they entered the temple early in the morning and taught.*
>
> *But when the officers came and did not find them in the prison, they returned and reported, saying, "Indeed we found the prison shut securely, and the guards standing outside before the doors; but when we opened them, we found no one inside!"*
>
> *So one came and told them, saying, "Look, the men whom you put in prison are standing in the temple and teaching the people!"*

Acts 5:17-21, 22-23, 25

The angel of the Lord came to not only free the apostles, but to instruct them to continue to speak words of life to the people. Their faithful preaching was the whole reason the persecution came. The apostles were preaching the gospel and the enemy came to steal the Word. This is why it is essential for a minister of God's Word to remain in the secret place of protection. If you are sharing the good news, then you are Satan's target. He has you in his crosshairs, his finger is on the trigger, and he is just looking for an opportunity to rain down destruction upon you. Nothing brings persecution quicker than preaching the gospel. The devil hates you and wants you to either keep quiet or die young. The devil tolerates religion but vehemently attacks anyone who spreads the good news of Jesus Christ.

The apostles were able to come out of the prison and return back to the temple undetected because of supernatural protection. When the high priest and officers found the disciples preaching in the temple, they threatened them, telling them to never preach the name or the blood of Jesus ever again: "Did we not strictly command you not to teach in this name? And look, you have filled Jerusalem with your doctrine, and intend to bring this Man's blood on us" (Acts 5:28). Peter fearlessly answered back that he and the other disciples would continue to preach the message of Jesus and the resurrection from the dead: "But Peter and the other apostles answered and said: 'We ought to obey God rather than men'" (Acts 5:29).

The high priest and Jewish leaders were furious at Peter and the other disciples and plotted to kill them (Acts 5:33). Gamaliel, a highly regarded Pharisee and teacher of the law, stood up and warned those who opposed the apostles that if the men were obeying God, then no one could stop them: "And now I say to you, keep away from these men and let them alone; for if this plan or this work is of men, it will come to nothing; but if it is of God, you cannot overthrow it—lest you even be found to fight against God" (Acts 5:38-39). Gamaliel recognized that the apostles' escape from prison was a sign of angelic protection and that no one could overthrow them.

Did you know that those who oppose you are not fighting against you but are fighting against God? There is no one bigger than the Most High. When you have God in your corner, you need not be afraid of anything or anyone. You know that His ministers of fire have charge over you.

Angelic Protection over God's Little Ones

Jesus warns not to mess with God's little ones who have angels guarding over them: "Take heed that you do not despise one of these little ones, for I say to you that in heaven their angels always see the face of My Father who is in heaven" (Matthew 18:10). Jesus laid hands on the little children and prayed over them

(Matthew 19:13-15). No doubt Jesus prayed angelic protection over the little children, knowing that it was the will of His Father that none of them should be destroyed.

God gives us assurance that the angels are assigned to protect God's little ones from being destroyed: "Even so it is not the will of your Father who is in heaven that one of these little ones should perish" (Matthew 18:14). Whether you are young or old, it is not the will of the Father for any of His children to perish.

Angelic Protection over Elisha

When Elisha the prophet was surrounded by a great Syrian army, he didn't cry out in fear, "Oh please have mercy on us! Don't kill me and my servant, I beg of you!" Elisha disregarded the army's threats and spoke to his servant, "Do not fear, for those who are with us are more than those who are with them" (2 Kings 6:16).

Elisha prayed for his servant and the Lord opened his eyes to see into the realm of the spirit. He saw what Elisha declared, that "there are more with us than those who are with them" (2 Kings 6:16). The servant looked around and saw the mountains filled with heavenly angels riding flaming horses and chariots (2 Kings 6:17). Remember what the Lord promised in the book of Zechariah? He promised to provide protection over His people with a wall of fire: "'For I,' says the LORD, 'will be a wall of fire all around her, and I will be the glory in her midst'" (Zechariah 2:5). The Lord protected Elisha and his servant with an angelic wall of fire. Can you imagine what that must have looked like? Just imagine, when you cover your family, your house, car, and place of business with the blood of Jesus and declare His protection, you are surrounded by an angelic wall of fire.

Elisha refused to fear when he saw that the Syrian army had surrounded him. Fear was the only thing that could have threatened Elisha and his servant. When Elisha refused to fear, suddenly, the entire Syrian army became visually impaired. The angelic host of heaven were empowered to act on the word spoken by Elisha and blinded the eyes of the Syrians (2 Kings 6:18).

Angel in Chapel Service

Have you ever wondered what angels really look like? I was a student at Oral Roberts University when an amazing event happened to me. I was in a very special chapel service, the first since President Oral Roberts returned back to campus after major heart surgery. Oral was the guest speaker and shared the three scriptures that had changed his life and ministry: John 10:10; Acts 10:38; and 3 John 2. While listening to the message, I was startled by the appearance of a huge man standing directly behind President Oral. The man's head was shrouded in white and his massive chest was several feet above President Oral's head. His body was completely covered in bright shining white clothing.

When I saw him, I closed my eyes in shock. I thought to myself, *What in the world did I just see?!!* I turned around to see if anyone else was freaking out. No one else looked puzzled except for me. I sat trembling in my seat. To be very honest, I had no desire at all to see an angel. In fact, I told the Lord while I sat trembling, "Why did You show me that Lord? You know I don't need to see an angel to believe they're real!"

At the end of the message, President Oral turned the service over to his son Richard. The first thing Richard Roberts said when he took to the platform was, "Dad, while you were ministering, I sensed a great presence of angels in this chapel service unlike I have ever felt before." Richard told us that while his dad was ministering, he noticed that the flags hanging above Oral's head were waving frantically. He acknowledged that this was a manifestation of the heavenly angels. The angel of God was watching over President Oral Roberts. Angels are very real and whether you see them or not, they have been following you all the days of your life. They have been commissioned by your Father to watch over you and they heed to His Word.

Angels Are Not Infants, Fairies, or Feminine

Unfortunately, religious tradition and entertainment has portrayed an erroneous picture of angels. The angels of God are not pretty women fairies wearing sparkling gowns. They are not adorable babies flying around with little wings or sitting on puffy clouds. The Bible does not make any mention of angels looking like this. The prophet Isaiah described the seraphim angels: "Each one had six wings: with two he covered his face, with two he covered his feet, and with two he flew" (Isaiah 6:2). That does not sound like any of the depictions of angels we see today.

So where did the idea that angels are dazzling females come from? The prophet Zechariah mentions seeing in his vision two women with wings: "Then I raised my eyes and looked, and there were two women, coming with the wind in their wings; for they had wings like the wings of a stork, and they lifted up the basket between earth and heaven" (Zechariah 5:9). The vision Zechariah saw of the two women with wings like the wings of a stork lifting up a basket represented the removal of wickedness from the land (Zechariah 5:5-8). The angel of the Lord never stated to Zechariah that the two women in the vision were angels. Never does the Bible refer to angels as female, but always in the male gender.

What about the idea that angels are little infants? Jesus did warn not to despise the children whose angels always see the face of their heavenly Father (Matthew 18:10), but Jesus did not teach that angels were like little children. The angels of heaven are mighty warriors who are equipped with great supernatural strength and power. One angel of the Lord struck down 185,000 Assyrian soldiers (2 Kings 19:35). That doesn't sound like a cute winged baby angel to me!

The Renaissance artists adapted these mythical, fairytale creatures into art and architecture and the trend has continued into modern day. But angels are not mythical creatures; they are real heavenly beings. The devil would love for us to think our angels are nothing more than cute, harmless babies with curly hair who play golden harps. The Bible tells us the truth about angels. They are only described as masculine,[19] as a spirit,[20] or as fire.[21] Angels are sent to minister for you and your family, to provide a fortress of fire all around you: "The angel of the LORD encamps all around those who fear Him, and delivers them" (Psalm 34:7).

Ministering Angels

The Bible says that some have unknowingly entertained angels: "Do not forget to entertain strangers, for by so doing some have unwittingly entertained angels" (Hebrews 13:2). That would mean you may have encountered an angel and didn't even know it.

When my wife was a teenager, she was out late bowling with her friend. She was on her way to drop her friend off at her house, which was located out near the everglades in an area known as "Alligator Ally." The roads in that area were gravel, narrow, and there were no street lights. It was just pitch black out there and there were lots of alligators. Lena's car suddenly started to blow steam out from under the hood, so she pulled over to the side of the road. Neither she nor her friend had any idea what to do and this was before there were cell phones. They were stuck out in the middle of "Alligator Ally" in the middle of the night with no nearby houses, no cars coming down the road, and they were miles from any pay phones.

One thing Lena knew to do was to pray. She learned this from her grandmother, who knew the power of prayer and the blood of Jesus. Lena started to pray over her and her friend as they sat in the car. All of a sudden, a man drove up and pulled to the side of the road. He didn't say anything like, "Hey are you alright?" or "Can I help you?" He just simply parked his car, got out and fixed Lena's car without asking her questions, and drove away. He never introduced himself and never asked for their names. He just showed up in the middle of the night with all the equipment needed to fix the car. Even though he looked like a normal man, he could have been an angel appearing as a man. That is why some may have unknowingly entertained angels.

Angels are sent forth to minister to those who will inherit salvation: "Are they not all ministering spirits sent forth to minister for those who will inherit salvation?" (Hebrews 1:14). When you were born again, you inherited not only eternal life but also angelic protection. You may look back and remember times when someone helped you and you never even knew who they were or where they came from. An angel may have helped you in the past and you didn't even know it.

Angels are not sent out to draw attention to themselves, but are sent to minister to those who are saved. That is why an angel will never tell you to worship him or to thank him for watching over you. When the Apostle John fell down to worship an angel, he was warned by the angel to only worship God: "See that you do not do that! I am your fellow servant, and of your brethren who have the testimony of Jesus" (Revelation 19:10). The angel was sent to serve John, not be worshipped.

Angels Excel in Strength

Bless the LORD, you His angels, who excel in strength, who do His word, heeding the voice of His word.

Psalm 103:20

How does an angel excel in strength? Does he work out at "God's Gym"? Psalm 103:20 tells us that when an angel heeds to the voice of God's Word, he excels in strength. Who gives voice to God's Word? You do. When you declare, "I will say of the LORD, He is my refuge and my fortress; my God, in Him I will trust" (Psalm 91:2), the angels excel in strength so they may heed to the voice of God's Word, to keep you in all your ways.

For He shall give His angels charge over you, to keep you in all your ways. In their hands they shall bear you up, lest you dash your foot against a stone.

Psalm 91:11-12

74

When you give voice to God's Word the angels of God are strengthened to do His good pleasure: "Bless the LORD, you His angels, who excel in strength, who do His word, heeding the voice of His word. Bless the LORD, all you His hosts, you ministers of His, who do His pleasure" (Psalm 103:20-21). When you give voice to God's Word, the angels of God encamp all around you to save you out of trouble: "This poor man cried out, and the LORD heard him, and saved him out of all his troubles. The angel of the LORD encamps all around those who fear Him, and delivers them" (Psalm 34:6-7).

When Zacharias prayed for a son, God heard his and his wife's prayers and sent a messenger angel. However, Zacharias did not believe the message and was speechless for nine months.

> *And Zacharias said to the angel, "How shall I know this? For I am an old man, and my wife is well advanced in years." And the angel answered and said to him, "I am Gabriel, who stands in the presence of God, and was sent to speak to you and bring you these glad tidings. But behold, you will be mute and not able to speak until the day these things take place, because you did not believe my words which will be fulfilled in their own time."*

> Luke 1:18-20

Notice that Gabriel told Zacharias why he would become speechless. It was because he did not believe the words of glad tidings. When you refuse to believe and speak the good news of supernatural protection, the angels will not excel in strength. They cannot heed to the voice of unbelief. They can only excel in strength as they heed to the voice of God's Word.

When Gabriel appeared to Mary, she gave voice to God's Word.

> *And having come in, the angel said to her, "Rejoice, highly favored one, the Lord is with you; blessed are you among women!"*

Then the angel said to her, "Do not be afraid, Mary, for you have found favor with God. And behold, you will conceive in your womb and bring forth a Son, and shall call His name JESUS...For with God nothing will be impossible."

Then Mary said, "Behold the maidservant of the Lord! Let it be to me according to your word." And the angel departed from her.

Luke 1:28, 30-31, 37-38

Notice that when Gabriel told Mary the glad tidings, she agreed with his words. This is what confession is all about - agreeing and saying the same thing God says in His Word. Mary was not struck speechless because she believed and gave voice to the words of glad tidings. When you believe and speak the good news of supernatural protection, the angels excel in strength and heed to God's Word.

Therefore we must give the more earnest heed to the things we have heard, lest we drift away. For if the word spoken through angels proved steadfast, and every transgression and disobedience received a just reward, how shall we escape if we neglect so great a salvation, which at the first began to be spoken by the Lord, and was confirmed to us by those who heard Him...For He has not put the world to come, of which we speak, in subjection to angels.

Hebrews 2:1-3, 5

When the Lord gave angels a message to speak, it was proved steadfast. The kingdom of God is not in subjection to angels but to us. We are the heirs of salvation. If you do not give voice to God's Word of supernatural protection, the angels are not able to heed and provide a way of escape.

The angels of the Lord are sent to keep you in the way you should go. When you believe and speak God's Word, the angels are strengthened to provide you deliverance. "Behold, I send an Angel before you to keep you in the way and to bring you into the place which I have prepared" (Exodus 23:20).

When you speak unbelief, the angel of the Lord cannot heed to the voice of God's Word. For example, if you are in the habit of saying, "I am scared to death that my child is going to get hurt on his skateboard," the angel cannot hearken to the voice of God's Word. You have spoken words of unbelief and rebellion. You may say, "WHAT! You mean to tell me that's rebellion? God knows what I mean! He understands my good intentions!" It may be true that you have good intentions, but it is still considered rebellion because a heart of unbelief is in rebellion.

> *Today, if you will hear His voice, do not harden your hearts as in the rebellion.*
>
> Hebrews 3:7-8

> *Beware, brethren, lest there be in any of you an evil heart of unbelief.*
>
> Hebrews 3:12

You may say, "But I do believe in God's protection. I'm just scared of my son getting hurt. The Lord knows my heart." That is true; God knows what you said is straight from your heart. Out of the abundance of the heart your mouth will speak (Matthew 12:34). Jesus tells us that we will give an account for every idle word which disagrees with Him (Matthew 12:36-37). Our words either agree with God or they disagree with God. There is no middle ground. You must get your mouth and heart in agreement with God's Word. When you declare, "The Lord is my refuge and my fortress. He watches over my son while he is on his skateboard. I cover him and the entire park with the blood of Jesus. My child is protected in Jesus' name," you have now empowered the angels to watch over your son.

When it comes to angels, there are no words that are "unintentional." When Zacharias disagreed in unbelief, Gabriel didn't say, "That's OK, Zach. I know what you really meant. I know what's in your heart." That's not at all what happened. Gabriel let Zach know on short notice, "I am Gabriel. I have been in the presence of God and I have a message for you...now be dumb and speechless till the promise has been fulfilled!"

You either agree with God's Word or you disagree with His Word. Exceptions are not made for good intentions. When you give voice to God's Word in faith, angels will watch over you every time. This is why we must "give the more earnest heed to the things we have heard, lest we drift away" (Hebrews 2:1). If we don't heed to God's Word, "how shall we escape if we neglect so great a salvation" (Hebrews 2:3)?

5TH KEY: YOU SHALL TRAMPLE UNDERFOOT

You shall tread upon the lion and the cobra, the young lion and the serpent you shall trample underfoot.

Psalm 91:13

I remember one time when my son was a little boy, he had just gotten out of bed and was standing in his pajamas when I noticed something moving near his feet. It was a snake! I quickly put on my hard-heel shoes and trampled the snake's head until it was crushed. As I stomped him, I said aloud to the snake, "I have authority over you and you will not come into my house and around my son!" I was reminded what the Lord said about trampling on the head of the serpent: "And I will put enmity between you and the woman, and between your seed and her Seed; He shall bruise your head, and you shall bruise His heel" (Genesis 3:15).

The fifth key of divine protection is stated in Psalm 91:13: "You shall tread upon the lion and the cobra, the young lion and the serpent you shall trample underfoot" (Psalm 91:13). You have authority to trample on the lion and the cobra, that is, the devil. The Hebrew word for "trample" is *ramac*, which means "to tread upon, stamp upon, to trample under feet." [22] You do not need to hide from the enemy; you can attack the enemy. You can march fiercely on the works of the devil.

Tread Upon the Lion

Belshazzar, whose name means "Bel Protect the King," [23] was the eldest son of the last Babylonian king, Nebuchadnezzar (Daniel 5:2). He held a great feast using the gold and silver vessels from the temple in Jerusalem. It was a direct violation for anyone, especially Gentiles, to touch the anointed vessels (Exodus 40:10). At the height of the feast, the finger of a man's hand appeared and wrote a message on the wall to warn Belshazzar. Daniel, the prophet of God, was brought before Belshazzar to interpret the inscription. Daniel reminded Belshazzar that his father, Nebuchadnezzar, had caused all peoples of all nations to tremble in fear of him and executed whomever he wished (Daniel 5:18-19). Daniel reminded Belshazzar that Nebuchadnezzar had been driven mad by the pride of his heart and pointed out that Belshazzar had not humbled his own heart (Daniel 5:21-23). Then Daniel interpreted the inscription's meaning. It was not good news for Belshazzar: "God has numbered your kingdom and finished it" (Daniel 5:26). That very night, Belshazzar was killed. The false god Bel was not able to protect Belshazzar's life.

Darius the Mede took the place of Belshazzar. Daniel continued to serve in the administration of the new king, Darius, who developed tremendous respect for Daniel. The governors and satraps were not happy about the relationship between Darius and Daniel and, unbeknownst to Darius, set out to trap Daniel so he could be killed. They convinced Darius to sign a decree that anyone who petitioned any god other than King Darius would be cast into the den of lions (Daniel 6:7). Daniel, knowing the decree, continued to openly give petitions to God. As a result, he was cast into the den of lions. Darius was distraught but assured Daniel saying, "Your God, whom you serve continually, He will deliver you" (Daniel 6:16).

Why would a Mede who did not know God make this statement? He must have known about Daniel's faith. Darius must have known that Daniel believed his God would deliver him, just as He had protected and delivered Daniel's three friends, Hananiah, Mishael, and Azariah. (Don't be concerned if you don't recognize these names. We will discuss them in a later chapter.)

Daniel did not expect to die when thrown into the den of lions. He fully expected the Angel of the Lord who delivered Hananiah, Mishael, and Azariah from the furnace to also deliver him from the den of lions. He was familiar with God's promises of divine protection: "You shall tread upon the lion and the cobra, the young lion and the serpent you shall trample underfoot" (Psalm 91:13).

Early the next morning, King Darius cried out to Daniel to see if his God had delivered him from death (Daniel 6:20). Daniel replied from the den of lions, "My God sent His angel and shut the lions' mouths, so that they have not hurt me, because I was found innocent before Him; and also, O king, I have done no wrong before you" (Daniel 6:22).

The king commanded that Daniel be taken out of the den. After examination, he was found to have no injury. The reason Daniel was delivered from death is clearly stated, "So Daniel was taken up out of the den, and no injury whatever was found on him, because he believed in his God" (Daniel 6:23). He was delivered from death because he believed his God would deliver him from the mouths of the lions. This is the same reason you can know you will be delivered from death. When you place your trust in the Lord, you will trample the lion and the cobra under your feet!

Save Me From the Lion's Mouth

David sang of how the Lord answered his call and delivered him from the enemy's sword and from wild beasts: "Deliver Me from the sword, my precious life from the power of the dog. Save me from the lion's mouth and from the horns of the wild oxen! You have answered me" (Psalm 22:20-21). David was delivered from the sword, the dog, the paw of the lion, the bear, and the heavyweight champion Goliath. How did David stay protected? He called on the Lord's blood covenant of protection: "Moreover David said, 'The LORD, who delivered me from the paw of the lion and from the paw of the bear, He will deliver me from the hand of this Philistine'" (1 Samuel 17:37). David said these words while facing death. He declared the Lord's deliverance while staring death in the face, just as Daniel, Hanahiah, Mishael, and Azariah did.

The mighty men who served under David also exercised their blood covenant over death: "Benaiah was the son of Jehoiada, the son of a valiant man from Kabzeel, who had done many deeds. He had killed two lion-like heroes of Moab. He had also gone down and killed a lion in the midst of a pit on a snowy day" (1 Chronicles 11:22).

The reason David and his men believed the Lord would protect them from death was because they had been taught the blood covenant of protection. They were familiar with the promises of Psalm 91. They understood their blood covenant with the God of Israel meant He would deliver them from anything that would try to harm them.

Dwell in Your Land Safely

According to Leviticus 26:22, Israel would suffer danger from wild animals if they did not follow the statutes of the Lord: "I will also send wild beasts among you, which shall rob you of your children, destroy your livestock, and make you few in number; and your highways shall be desolate." If Israel followed the Lord's statutes, they would be granted peace and protection in the land: "(You shall) dwell in your land safely. I will give peace in the land and you shall lie down, and none will make you afraid; I will rid the land of evil (or wild) beasts, and the sword will not go through your land" (Leviticus 26:5-6, explanations mine).

During our outreaches in the inner cities of South Florida, our outreach team encountered some pretty intimidating dogs. Before each outreach, we would cover the neighborhoods with the blood of Jesus and agree together for divine protection. Many of the people living in the neighborhoods had guard dogs like German shepherds, Rottweilers, and Pitbulls. Just as the Lord kept Israel safe from the violent men and animals of Egypt, He kept our outreach team safe and He will do the same for you.

> *But against none of the children of Israel shall a dog move its tongue, against man or beast, that you may know that the LORD does make a difference between the Egyptians and Israel.*

> Exodus 11:7

Once my daughter and I were walking next to a house and a German shepherd came running up next to us. I told Hannah, "Don't be afraid. The angels of the Lord are encamped around us and this dog will not even bark at us." We both witnessed how the German shepherd just sniffed us, wagged its tail, and everything was cool. When you are surrounded by the angels of God, even the wild animals know and will be at peace with you.

> *For you shall have a covenant with the stones of the field, and the beasts of the field shall be at peace with you.*

> Job 5:23

When you activate the blood covenant of divine protection, you'll witness for yourself miraculous acts of God. You may never encounter a lion except at the city zoo, but there may be a time when you encounter someone with a weapon or a ferocious dog snarling at you. You have a promise from the Lord that you can dwell in your land safely. This promise is not based on the condition of your living in a "safe" neighborhood. Any neighborhood is safe when you are dwelling in the secret place of the Most High.

Dominion Over All the Earth

You activate the blood covenant of protection by placing your trust in the blood of Jesus Christ and declaring by faith, "He is my refuge, my fortress, He is my God and in Him I will trust" (Psalm 91:2). Words spoken from your heart in faith release the power of God's blood covenant of supernatural protection. The angels of God respond to the Lord's blood covenant of protection when words of faith are spoken directly from your born-again spirit.

God made man in His image and gave him dominion over all the earth.

> *Then God said, "Let Us make man in Our image, according to Our likeness; let them have dominion over the fish of the sea, over the birds of the air, and over the cattle, over all the earth and over every creeping thing that creeps on the earth."*

Genesis 1:26

The Hebrew word translated "God" in this verse is *Elohim*. Elohim is plural, giving reference to the Godhead (Romans 1:20; Colossians 2:9). The Godhead came together and discussed man's purpose in life. When the Father, Son, and Holy Spirit decided to make man in "Our image" and "Our likeness" to "have dominion over all the earth," it was settled. No one can stop kidnapping, sex trafficking, gang rape, terrorism, mass murders, or drive by shootings except the Church. No one can stop tornados, earthquakes, tsunamis, flooding, and hurricanes except the Church. When God decided to put man in charge, the Body of Christ was given dominion.

If you are going to operate in the blessing of Psalm 91, it is essential for you to understand your dominion on the earth. Your heavenly Father promises to protect you and your family from all danger, no matter how dark the world may be. It is the will of the Father for you to live your life covered by His blood, abiding safe in His hiding place of protection.

When man sinned in the garden, he forfeited his dominion in the earth; but Jesus' sacrifice on the cross restored to man his dominion. Through faith in His Word, His name, and His blood, we have been given dominion over all the power of the enemy and nothing shall by any means hurt us (Luke 10:19). We are seated in Christ in heavenly places with the devil underneath our feet.

In Ephesians 1:15-23, the Apostle Paul prayed for the believers to receive a revelation understanding of their dominion. Father God has put all things under the feet of Christ and has given to the Church His dominion and power. All things that are under the feet of Jesus are underneath your feet. You can boldly stand against every attack of the enemy, knowing you are seated in Christ far above all principality, power, might, and dominion.

The Ephesians 1:15-23 prayer can be personalized so you can pray and receive by faith the wisdom and revelation understanding of your dominion in Christ. I encourage you to use this prayer and receive this revelation for yourself.

> *Father, may You give to me the spirit of wisdom and revelation in the knowledge of You.*
>
> *May the eyes of my understanding be enlightened; may I know what is the hope of Your calling, may I know what are the riches of the glory of Your inheritance, and may I know the exceeding greatness of Your power toward me who believes, according to the working of Your mighty power which You worked in Christ when You raised Him from the dead and seated Him at Your right hand in the heavenly places, far above all principality and power and*

might and dominion, and every name that is named, not only in this age but also in that which is to come.

You have put all things under His feet, and gave Him to be head over all things to the Church, which is His body, the fullness of Him who fills all in all. In Jesus' name. Amen.

Rejoice in the Dance

For several months, both of my legs were very weak and in much pain. I was seen by specialists who could not figure out what was wrong. One Saturday morning, I woke up and that was it…I'd had enough. I declared boldly, "I am getting out of this bed and going to get my healing!" Then the Lord asked me, "I thought you said you were already healed?" I knew He was right and I was wrong. I had been confessing, "I am healed by the stripes of Jesus," yet I was still waiting for a manifestation before I would rejoice.

Let me give you a quick quiz before we go any further. Base your answer on what you believe the Bible teaches.

When should you rejoice?

      A. Before the miracle

      B. During the miracle

      C. After the miracle

So what's your answer? If your answer is A, you are correct. Before you see anything happen, you should rejoice for the miracle. If your answer is B, you are also correct. Always give praise while you are experiencing the miracle. If your answer is C, you are correct as well. You should always give thanks after the miracle has manifested. So the answer would actually be: D. "All of the above."

Israel, who wandered around in the wilderness, would have answered "C." They would rejoice in the Lord only after the miracle manifested. When Israel needed a miracle, they didn't praise God; they persecuted Moses saying, "Because there were no graves in Egypt, have you taken us away to die in the wilderness?" (Exodus 14:11). When Israel was crossing the Red Sea, they still did not give God praise. It was only after they crossed the Red Sea and saw their Egyptian pursuers drown in the waters that they sang the song of Moses, "The LORD is my strength and song, and He has become my salvation" (Exodus 15:2). Moses' sister Miriam and the women of Israel broke out in song and dance only after they had walked across the Red Sea and onto dry ground: "Sing to the LORD, for He has triumphed gloriously! The horse and its rider He has thrown into the sea" (Exodus 15:21). But the song of Moses and the song of Miriam should have been sung before, during, and after the miracle of crossing the Red Sea. That is how you tread on the lion and the cobra - you praise, rejoice, and dance before, during, and after the manifestation.

The way to trample on the enemy is to have praise continually in your mouth and in your feet. Don't just dance and rejoice when the bills are paid and your body and emotions are feeling good. You trample on the lion and the cobra when you rejoice in the Lord always: "Rejoice in the Lord always. Again I will say, rejoice" (Philippians 4:4). Paul wrote those words from a Roman prison! So when should you rejoice and dance? Rejoice in the Lord always, always, always..and again I say, rejoice, rejoice, rejoice!

As I sat in bed with both legs in pain that day, I meditated on what the Lord said to me: "I thought you said you were already healed?" I answered the Lord, "You're right! I am healed!" He then asked me, "So what should you do if you are healed right now?" I answered, "Jump out of bed!" So I did. I jumped out of bed and landed on the hard wood floor in my bare feet. The pain shot through both of my legs into my whole body. I didn't pay any attention. I rejoiced in the dance in my bare feet all through the house. I did every dance I could think of. I danced the Hora, the Cossack…I even danced like MC Hammer! I danced for thirty minutes all over the house while both of my legs were in great pain. Then all of a sudden, the pain completely left my body and it never came back!

> *Then shall the virgin rejoice in the dance, and the young men and the old, together; for I will turn their mourning to joy, will comfort them, and make them rejoice rather than sorrow. I will satiate the soul of the priests with abundance, and My people shall be satisfied with My goodness, says the LORD.*

> Jeremiah 31:13-14

The way to trample on the devil is to rejoice always in the Lord. When you rejoice in the dance, when you feel like mourning, He will turn your sorrow into joy.

CHAPTER 8

6ᵀᴴ KEY: YOU HAVE SET YOUR LOVE UPON HIM

The sixth key to divine protection is found in Psalm 91, verse 14, "Because he has set his love upon Me, therefore I will deliver him." These words reveal the love relationship the psalmist had with God and the trust he put in God as his unfailing place of refuge.

In the Amplified Bible, verse 14 reads, "Because he has set his love upon Me, therefore will I deliver him; I will set him on high, because he knows and understands My name [has a personal knowledge of My mercy, love, and kindness - trusts and relies on Me, knowing I will never forsake him, no, never]" (AMPC). The psalmist's personal knowledge of the Father's mercy, love, and kindness gave him assurance that he would be delivered from trouble. Why do we set our love upon God? Because He set His love upon us first: "But God demonstrates His own love toward us, in that while we were still sinners, Christ died for us" (Romans 5:8). You cannot love Him unless you know He loves you first - unconditionally.

Beloved of the Lord

Before Moses died, he pronounced a blessing over the twelve tribes of Israel (Deuteronomy 33). Moses spoke over the tribe of Benjamin that they were the beloved of the Lord and would dwell in the safety of His shelter all day long: "Of Binyamin he said: 'Adonai's beloved lives securely. He protects him day after day. He lives between his shoulders'" (Deuteronomy 33:12, CJB).

The Hebrew name "Benjamin" means, "Son of the south, son of the right hand." [24] Remember what we learned in the Ephesians 1:15-23 prayer? You are right now seated in Christ at the right hand of the Father (Ephesians 1:20). You are the beloved son of the right hand. As you set your love upon the Father, you will experience His loving protection and live free from the fear of any danger.

John the Beloved

The Apostle John described himself as the disciple "whom Jesus loved" (John 21:20). He also identified himself as the disciple "who also had leaned on His breast at the supper" (John 21:20). John spoke of Jesus' love for him five times in his gospel (John 13:23; 19:26; 20:2; 21:7; 21:20). But his unique identification of himself as the one "whom Jesus loved" was not meant to compare him with the other disciples; it was a reflection of his intimate relationship with Jesus. John had a revelation understanding of the love of Christ. He believed and received the love of Christ for him. John knew that Jesus loved him.

It is vitally important for you to know you are deeply loved by your heavenly Father. I'm sure you would agree that John 3:16 is probably the most famous, well-known verse in the Bible: "For God so loved the world that He gave His only begotten Son, that whoever believes in Him should not perish but have everlasting life." That scripture is talking about you! God loves you so much that He gave His greatest gift, His only Son, to die for you on the cross. Notice that it was the disciple whom Jesus loved, the one who received a revelation of the love of Christ, who wrote John 3:16.

When you know you are loved by Jesus, it makes you fearless. John testified to this when he wrote, "There is no fear in love; but perfect love casts out fear, because fear involves torment. But he who fears has not been made perfect in love" (1 John 4:18). You may ask, "Who in the world could know perfect love?" You can! The love of God has been shed abroad in your heart by the Holy Spirit. His perfect love is inside of you (Romans 5:5).

John lived in a very dangerous time when the church was heavily persecuted all over the world. He displayed fearlessness by being the only disciple present at the crucifixion of Jesus (John 19:26). When John was thrown into boiling oil before the Latin Gate in Rome, he survived without any recorded injury. The Roman Emperor Domitian banished John to the Island of Patmos, a small island located in the Mediterranean Sea where enemies of Rome were incarcerated. During his banishment, John was protected from other prisoners and wild beasts because he remained underneath the shadow of the Almighty. From Patmos, he wrote "The Revelation of Jesus Christ." Following his time on Patmos, John went back to Ephesus (modern day Turkey), where he lived to be a very old man.

Leaned on His Breast

Then Peter, turning around, saw the disciple whom Jesus loved following who also had leaned on His breast at the supper…seeing him, said to Jesus, "But Lord, what about this man?" Jesus said to him, "If I will that he remain till I come, what is that to you? You follow Me."

John 21:20-22

Notice two things mentioned here to characterize John's intimate relationship with Jesus: He was the disciple whom Jesus loved and he leaned on Jesus' chest during the Passover supper. What makes these two things so important as to merit mention?

We know John consistently identified himself as the "disciple whom Jesus loved." Did Jesus tell John he was His favorite? I'm sure He did not. Do you think Jesus assured all His disciples He loved them? Of course He did! We know that He is no respecter of persons and has no favorites. The Apostle Peter declared that he perceived that God shows no partiality (Acts 10:34). Jesus made certain that His disciples knew they were all loved: "The Father Himself loves you" (John 16:27). But it was John, the youngest of the twelve, who received a personal revelation, "My Jesus loves me!"

John was the only disciple during the Passover dinner who felt comfortable enough to lean on Jesus' chest. I can't say that I've ever felt so warm around another minister that I leaned on top of his chest. But we can have such closeness with Jesus that we can sit at His feet or even crawl up in His lap and bask in His presence without any sense of awkwardness, guilt, shame, or inferiority.

The gospels show us what Jesus was really like while He was on earth. He was loving, kind, and approachable. He did not make you feel like you were not good enough to be in the same room with Him. Jesus never made the hurting and broken feel like they were an annoyance and unwelcome. Everyone wanted to have Jesus over for dinner. Only the prideful, arrogant, religious dignitaries disliked Him. Jesus demonstrated to all of us that we are His beloved.

Beloved Brethren

Throughout the New Testament epistles, believers are referred to as "beloved." The apostles frequently identified their fellow brothers and sisters in Christ as "beloved," "beloved of God," or "beloved brethren."

Beloved, now we are children of God.

1 John 3:2

Beloved, if God so loved us, we also ought to love one another.

1 John 4:11

Beloved, I pray that you may prosper in all things and be in health, just as your soul prospers.

3 John 2

When Jesus was baptized in water, the Holy Spirit rested on Him and the voice of the Father declared, "You are My beloved Son, in whom I am well pleased" (Mark 1:11). The Father, Son, and Holy Spirit were all in agreement that Jesus is the "Beloved Son." When you receive Jesus as your Lord and Savior by the glory of God's grace, His unmerited favor, you are accepted as His beloved. In Christ, you are made a beloved child and are recognized by the Father, Son, and Holy Spirit as the beloved of God. "To the praise of the glory of His grace, by which He made us accepted in the Beloved" (Ephesians 1:6).

When you know you are accepted in the Beloved, it causes you to set your love upon Him. The one who sets his love upon the Lord shall be delivered: "Because he has set his love upon Me, therefore I will deliver him" (Psalm 91:14). The one who sets his love upon the Father knows he can trust in the Father's protection. When you declare, "He is my refuge and my fortress; My God, in Him I will trust," your declaration of the Lord's protection shows you have a Father-son relationship with the Lord. God is not an impersonal Creator who has distanced Himself from you. God is your refuge, He is your fortress, He is your Father. You know you will be preserved underneath the shadow of His protection: "The LORD preserves all who love Him" (Psalm 145:20). You have set your love upon Him because you know Him as Abba, Father (Romans 8:15).

A Father's Love

When I was in elementary school, I had a very hard time concentrating. My grades were poor because I didn't pay attention to the teacher. I was known as the class clown and would make strange noises and silly faces while the teacher was trying to teach. My dad asked the teacher, "Why don't you reprimand my son when he interrupts your class?" The teacher answered, "Because he's so cute and funny!" That did not help me at all.

Then the teacher informed my dad that I had not done my homework for the entire year. I only had one month to make up the work, or I would be held back. You could say that I was in deep "poo-doo"! My dad asked the teacher, "Didn't you ever give a deadline for my son to complete his homework?" The teacher answered, "I always tell my students to work at their own pace."

My dad met with me and asked, "Brian, why have you not been doing your homework all year?" My answered echoed what the teacher said: "I'm working at my own pace." Dad did not find my answer humorous. Every night, I was confined to my room while I did all the homework that was assigned for the entire year – all in one month! Every day, including weekends, I was locked in my room doing nothing but homework, homework, and more homework. I learned my multiplication tables in that month. I was dreaming the multiplication tables. I had them for breakfast, lunch, afternoon snack, and dinner. If it hadn't been for my dad working with me, I would have been held back and not learned anything in elementary school except how to entertain the classroom.

When I saw my dad working with me every night, I knew he really cared. If he didn't care, he would not have bothered to help me. He would have said, "It's your own fault you flunked the third grade!" But instead of condemning me, he showed me love. In one month's time, I was able to finish a year's worth of homework and passed the grade.

A father's love can persuade a child that he or she can do anything, no matter the odds. Even if the child messes up, they believe they can still overcome. If a child believes for a moment that mom or dad is against them, many times they will simply dig their heels in and refuse to budge. Children need to believe their parents are for them and not against them. A parent's love greatly impacts a child's attitude and behavior.

He Is for You, Not Against You

Your heavenly Father is for you, not against you. There is nothing you have done that can separate you from the Father's love. The Apostle Paul says in Romans 8:31, "What then shall we say to these things? If God is for us, who can be against us?" Paul starts with a good question. What do you say about your Father when you're in a mess and it's your own dumb fault? Paul tells us what we should say in response to anything we are facing – no matter what, if God is for us, who can be against us? The Apostle Paul goes on to further explain the love our Father has for us.

He who did not spare His own Son, but delivered Him up for us all, how shall He not with Him also freely give us all things?

Yet in all these things we are more than conquerors through Him who loved us.

Romans 8:32, 37

When you believe that God your Father is for you and not against you, it will cause you to overcome anything and everything. You are more than a conqueror in Him who loves you. No matter how big a mess you may be facing, no matter who is out to get you, know this and know it well - if Father God is for you, then who or what can be against you?

If Father God was willing to give His own Son to make you His child, how much more freely will He give you all things? I know this may sound too amazing to be true. That is why you must meditate on Romans 8:31-39 until you have it written on the tablet of your heart.

On the other hand, if you believe God is against you, then anyone and anything will hurt you all the time. It will be true of you, "If anything can go wrong, it will." It will seem that everyone is always picking on you and everyone takes advantage of you. This can only be cured by the love of God. You have to believe His love for you. His deliverance will come when you set your love upon Him, knowing that He is for you and not against you.

The Love and Blood Connection

Yet in all things we are more than conquerors through Him who loved us. For I am persuaded that neither death nor life, nor angels nor principalities nor powers, nor things present nor things to come, nor height nor depth, nor any other created thing, shall be able to separate us from the love of God which is in Christ Jesus our Lord.

Romans 8:37-39

When you believe and receive the love God has for you, it will cause you to set your love upon your heavenly Father. The blood of Jesus is God's love poured out for you. His precious blood is what justifies you and declares you, "Not guilty!" No one can bring a charge against you in the heavenly courthouse when you plead the blood. You cannot be separated from God's love because His blood has made you righteous. Can you see the love and blood connection here? As long as your faith is in His love and in His blood, then nothing will be able to separate you from Him.

What color do you associate with love? Beige? Indigo? Emerald? I'm sure you, like everyone else, associate red with the thought of love. It's no mistake that both love and blood are associated with the same color. When you cover yourself with

Christ's blood, you are covering yourself with His love. Nothing can cross the blood line of Jesus, and nothing can separate you from the love of Jesus.

I want to share the following prayer based on Ephesians 3:14-21 that I believe will help you immensely in receiving insight into God's amazing love. I encourage you to pray this prayer aloud and personalize it as you set your love upon Him.

> *Father, I ask that You grant me according to the riches of Your glory that I would be strengthened with might through Your Spirit in my inner man.*
>
> *Jesus, may You dwell richly in my heart through faith.*
>
> *May I be rooted and grounded in Your love, able to comprehend what is the width and length and depth and height of the love of Christ. Fill me with all of Your fullness.*
>
> *Now to You, Father, who is able to do in my life exceedingly, abundantly above all that I could ask or think, according to the power that is working in me now, to You be all the glory forever and ever.*
>
> *Amen.*

Abiding in the Father's Love

To gain a deeper understanding of the Father's love, do an in-depth study of the Gospel of John and the epistle of First John. The more you understand the Father's love, the more your intimacy with Him will grow. God doesn't have love, He is love. He does not love you for who you are, but because of who He is. Father God is love.

And we have known and believed the love that God has for us. God is love, and he who abides in love abides in God, and God in him.

1 John 4:16

Anytime you walk in the love of God, you are abiding in the secret place of protection. The wicked one cannot touch you when you abide in God's love, covered by His blood: "We know that whoever is born of God does not sin; but he who has been born of God keeps himself, and the wicked one does not touch him" (1 John 5:18). This is why Jesus was protected all the time He was on earth. The wicked one could not touch Jesus because He abided in His Father's love. When you abide in the Father's love, you keep His commandments and the wicked one cannot touch you.

Abide in Me, and I in you. As the branch cannot bear fruit of itself, unless it abides in the vine, neither can you, unless you abide in Me. I am the vine, you are the branches. He who abides in Me, and I in him, bears much fruit; for without Me you can do nothing.

John 15:4-5

Jesus points out that you cannot produce the fruit of love without abiding in Him. This is because He is the vine, and you're not. Only when you abide in Jesus will you be able to love like Jesus and forgive like Jesus. You are a branch and cannot produce fruit on your own. But when you abide in Him, engaging in intimate fellowship, you practice His presence and bear the same fruit He did. Fellowship with Him from the moment you awaken until the sun goes down. Pray without ceasing. There is no other way to abide in the love of the Father and produce fruit except to abide in the vine of Jesus.

As the Father loved Me, I also have loved you; abide in My love. If you keep My commandments you will abide in My

*love, just as I have kept My Father's commandments and
abide in His love.*

John 15:9-10

*This is My commandment, that you love one another as I
have loved you. Greater love has no one than this, than to
lay down one's life for his friends.*

John 15:12-13

We are commanded to love one another, even the brethren.
Sometimes it is harder to love the brethren than to love sinners.
Why? We expect sinners to act like sinners, but we expect the
brethren to act like Christians. Part of loving one another is
forgiving when we have been wronged. You may have been
wounded in the past; forgiveness is how you heal. Forgiveness is a
choice that only *you* can make. When you choose to forgive, you
are abiding in the Vine.

This is one of the reasons we are not to forsake the assembling
of ourselves together as the Day is approaching, so we may love
the brethren: "And let us consider one another in order to stir up
love and good works, not forsaking the assembling of ourselves
together, as is the manner of some, but exhorting one another, and
so much the more as you see the Day approaching" (Hebrews
10:24-25). When you stir up love for the brethren, you are loving
them unconditionally just like your Father has loved you
unconditionally. If you avoid assembling together and have no
church that you call your spiritual home, then how can you love
the brethren? You stir up love for the brethren by deciding to
assemble yourselves together. This is how God designed for us to
increase and mature in His love for one another.

*He who says, "I know Him", and does not keep His
commandments, is a liar, and the truth is not in him. But*

whoever keeps His word, truly the love of God is perfected (or matured) in him. By this we know that we are in Him.

1 John 2:4-5, explanation mine

He who says he is in the light, and hates his brother, is in darkness until now. He who loves his brother abides in the light, and there is no cause for stumbling in him.

1 John 2:9-10

The wicked one cannot touch you when you are walking in the light of love. When you walk out of love, you are in darkness and will stumble. Stay out of darkness and abide in the light by abiding in the Father's love.

CHAPTER 9

7TH KEY: YOU HAVE KNOWN HIS NAME

I will set him on high, because he has known My name.

Psalm 91:14

The seventh key to divine protection given in Psalm 91 is to know God's name. The Lord assured the psalmist that He would set him high above the storm of trouble and shelter him under His wings because he knew God's name. God revealed His name as Yahweh.

> *Then Moses said to God, "Indeed, when I come to the children of Israel and say to them, 'The God of your fathers has sent me to you,' and they say to me, 'What is His name?' what shall I say to them?" And God said to Moses, "I AM WHO I AM." And He said, "Thus you shall say to the children of Israel, 'I AM has sent me to you.'" Moreover God said to Moses, "Thus you shall say to the children of Israel: 'The LORD God of your fathers, the God*

of Abraham, the God of Isaac, and the God of Jacob, has sent me to you. This is My name forever, and this is My memorial to all generations.'"

Exodus 3:13-15

The name I AM signifies "I AM who always was, I AM who always is, and I AM who always shall be." The Israelites referred to I AM by the Hebrew consonants YHWH, a name so sacred, they believed it should never be said aloud. Instead, they would substitute the word *Adonai* in place of the sacred tetragrammaton. Eventually, Jewish rabbinical scholars inserted the vowels from Adonai between the Hebrew consonants to form the word, Yahweh.[25]

The angel of the Lord revealed to Joseph the name to be given to the Son of God: "And she will bring forth a Son, and you shall call His name JESUS" (Matthew 1:21). The angel Gabriel revealed His name to Mary: "And behold, you will conceive in your womb and bring forth a Son, and shall call His name JESUS" (Luke 1:31). Through faith in His blood, we have been given the legal right and privilege to pronounce and declare the holy and majestic name of Jesus. Mankind has been given the sacred name of Jesus, which provides eternal salvation: "And you shall call His name JESUS, for He will save His people from their sins" (Matthew 1:21).

The name "Jesus" comes from the Hebrew name "Joshua." Moses called Hoshea, the son of Nun, "Yeshuwa" (Numbers 13:16), which means "YHWY is salvation." [26] The name Jesus, used in the New Testament, is a Greek transliteration of the Hebrew name Yeshuwa.[27] When we use the name of Jesus by faith, we are calling out, "YHWH is our salvation, our deliverance, and our protection." We find refuge in knowing His name.

The name of Adonai is a strong tower; a righteous person runs to it and is raised high [above danger].

Proverbs 18:10, CJB

Our Legal Right

Jesus gave His disciples the legal right to use His name: "And in that day you will ask Me nothing. Most assuredly I say to you, whatever you ask the Father in My name He will give you. Until now you have asked nothing in My name. Ask, and you will receive that your joy may be full" (John 16:23-24).

When Jesus said, "In that day you will ask Me nothing," He was referring to the day of the new covenant in which we now live, when believers can approach God as Father based on the authority of the name of Jesus and His blood. The authority to approach God as Father lies in the use of Jesus' name, not our own ability. If you have been born again, you have been given a legal right to use the name that is above every power in heaven, earth, and beneath the earth.

Every time I sign on my home computer, I must first type in the password. If I don't type in the password correctly, I will not have access to the benefits of the computer. When you ask for something from the Father, it must be endorsed in the name of Jesus. When you ask for anything in Jesus' name, His name validates it and the Father provides it. You have been given the "secret password" that links you to the Father's unlimited ability and resources.

Dominion in the Name of Jesus

The name of Jesus gives us the ability to exercise dominion over every name that is named: "Therefore God also has highly exalted Him and given Him the name which is above every name" (Philippians 2:9). This would include every disease with names

103

like "cancer," every terrorist group with names like "ISIS," and every natural disaster with names like "Hurricane Katrina." If it has a name, the name of Jesus is above it!

When the seventy disciples returned to Jesus, they were overjoyed of how demons shuddered at the name of Jesus.

> *Then the seventy returned with joy, saying, "Lord, even the demons are subject to us in Your name." And He said to them, "I saw Satan fall like lightning from heaven. Behold, I give you the authority to trample on serpents and scorpions, and over all the power of the enemy, and nothing shall by any means hurt you."*

Luke 10:17-19

Notice that the authority given to us when we use Jesus' name trumps all the works of the devil. We don't just have "some" authority over "some" powers. We have authority over ALL the power of the enemy. Jesus likens this dominion over the enemy to trampling over serpents and scorpions.

Above Every Name

In the Bible, the devil is referred to by such names as "prince of the power of the air" (Ephesians 2:2), "god of this world" (2 Corinthians 4:4), "serpent" (2 Corinthians 11:3), "dragon" (Revelation 12:3), and "a roaring lion" (1 Peter 5:8). When you use the name of Jesus, you trample over all the works of the destroyer. This includes every evil spirit that is embodied as a serpent, scorpion, dragon, and lion: "You shall tread upon the lion and the cobra, the young lion and the serpent you shall trample underfoot" (Psalm 91:13). There is not one name - including Satan's name - that is greater than Jesus' name. The name of Jesus is greater and is above every other name.

Keys to Death, Hell, and the Grave

Hell is neither the devil's headquarters nor his warehouse. Satan no longer has the keys to death, hell, and the grave as he did before the cross (Matthew 16:19; Revelation 1:18). We have been given *eternal life* and devils have on reserve in hell *everlasting chains* (Jude 6). When Jesus appeared to John on the isle of Patmos, He stated that He has the keys of dominion over all death, hell, and the grave (Revelation 1:18). Jesus authorized the Church to exercise His dominion on the earth: "All authority has been given to Me in heaven and on earth. Go therefore … and lo, I am with you always, even to the end of the age" (Matthew 28:18-20).

Jesus sent us into the world with the keys of dominion over ALL things on the earth, which includes all of its elements. We have been given dominion over rain, wind, fire, hail, and storms. When we exercise dominion on the earth in the name of Jesus, power is released as if Jesus Himself spoke.

Subdue the Earth and Keep It

God did not keep the Garden of Eden. God gave Adam the obligation to tend and keep the Garden of Eden, to cultivate it and subdue it (Genesis 2:15). In other words, God created man to have dominion on the earth and to rule over it as king of God's creation. God's sovereign design is for humanity to have dominion over planet earth. If Adam had protected his wife from the serpent, Eve would have never been deceived. But because of Adam's failure to exercise his responsibility to keep the Garden of Eden, he and his wife suffered misfortune. Why was the serpent able to deceive Eve, God's beautiful and innocent creation? Adam forsook his responsibility to guard Eve.

God ordained man to be ruler over everything on the earth (Genesis 1:26). When man fell into sin, he lost his dominion over the earth. Jesus came to reverse the curse and bring dominion back to man. Jesus "upholds all things by the word of His power" (Hebrews 1:3). He taught His disciples that if they did what He taught, they would be unshakable - like a man who digs deep to lay the foundation of his house on a rock.

Whoever comes to Me, and hears My sayings and does them, I will show you whom he is like: He is like a man building a house, who dug deep and laid the foundation on the rock. And when the flood arose, the stream beat vehemently against that house, and could not shake it, for it was founded on the rock.

Luke 6:47-48

Shalom in the Storm

The disciples saw Jesus exhibit unshakable faith during a storm. Jesus and His disciples were in a boat traveling across the Sea of Galilee, which is about thirteen miles long and eight miles wide.[28] A great storm suddenly arose and covered the boat with waves (Matthew 8:23-24). The gospel of Mark says of this great tempest, "And a great windstorm arose, and the waves beat into the boat" (Mark 4:37).

During this great storm, Jesus remained asleep. It may be that Jesus was exhausted, but no doubt He was soaked from the rain and waves. Jesus was at peace during a torrential storm, knowing that He was in the secret place of His Father's protection.

The disciples woke Jesus saying, "Teacher, do You not care that we are perishing" (Mark 4:38). They were full of fear because they had not set their love upon Him. They questioned His love, thinking that He would rather sleep than save them. Jesus first addressed the fear in their hearts, "Why are you fearful, O you of little faith" (Matthew 8:26). Jesus was demonstrating to the disciples that they had no reason to be afraid. He loved them unconditionally. They only needed to exercise their dominion over the storm using His name.

The disciples should have been familiar with Psalm 46, which promises the Father's protection from the power of the sea.

> *God is our refuge and strength, a very present help in trouble. Therefore we will not fear, even though the earth be removed, and though the mountains be carried into the midst of the sea; though its waters roar and be troubled, though the mountains shake with its swelling. Selah.*

Psalm 46:1-3

Jesus had the promises of protection written on the tablet of His heart before the storm came. This is why Jesus was able to rest and be unafraid in the midst of the raging storm. When the storm came, Jesus was already full of faith rather than full of fear. He was abiding in His Father's love. The love of the Father kept Him at ease in peaceful rest. Jesus had already built His house on the foundation of His Father's love and on His Word (Luke 6:47-48). This is how you can rest in the midst of a storm. When you feed on the Father's Word and His love, your home will experience shalom, even in the midst of a storm.

Speak to the Storm

Jesus exercised dominion over the storm by speaking to it. The disciples expected Jesus to step in and rescue them, "Teacher, do You not care that we are perishing" (Mark 4:38). Jesus did not pray to the Father, He spoke directly to the storm. He did not pray for divine protection but exercised dominion over the storm by saying to the wind and sea, "Peace, be still" (Mark 4:39). Jesus had assurance of His Father's protection before the wind ever started to blow. He knew He was in the shelter of the Almighty, so all that needed to be done was to exercise His dominion over the storm.

After Jesus took dominion over the storm, the disciples said one to another, "Who can this be, that even the wind and sea obey Him" (Mark 4:41). They were unaware that the dominion Jesus exercised over the earth was the same dominion He has given to those who believe in His name (Mark 16:15-18). The disciples needed to exercise their dominion over storms, knowing that Jesus was always with them. They believed the winds and sea obeyed Jesus, but did not believe the winds and sea would obey Jesus' name. The winds and the sea would have obeyed the disciples if they had exercised their dominion in Jesus' name.

On another occasion, Jesus instructed His disciples to get into a boat and meet Him on the other side (Matthew 14:22). He then went up the mountain alone to pray (Matthew 14:23). Not long into the disciples' short journey, a sudden windstorm came blowing contrary to the direction they were headed (Matthew 14:24). The disciples struggled against the storm for at least nine hours until the fourth watch of the night just before dawn, then they saw Jesus walking on the water and they were greatly troubled and cried out in fear (Matthew 14:26).

When Jesus stepped into the boat, the windstorm immediately ceased (Matthew 14:32). Why didn't the windstorm cease before Jesus stepped into the boat? The disciples did not understand the dominion that was theirs when using the name of Jesus. Jesus was confident, even in the windstorm, because He had made Father God His place of refuge and shelter. The disciples' fear of death could have been averted had they meditated on the promises of protection that were theirs: "If I take the wings of the morning, and dwell in the uttermost parts of the sea, even there Your hand shall lead me, and Your right hand shall hold me" (Psalm 139:9-10).

So how does this apply to you? You have authority to use the name of Jesus to speak to storms, flood waters, and destructive winds and they will obey you: "You rule the raging of the sea; when its waves rise, You still them" (Psalm 89:9). That is what Jesus was showing His disciples – how to take dominion on the earth. You are not exercising dominion by talking about the storm. You have to speak to the storm and it will obey you in Jesus' name: "He calms the storm, so that its waves are still. Then they are glad because they are quiet; so He guides them to their desired haven" (Psalm 107:29-30).

Teenage Boys Exercised Their Dominion

Once I was invited to speak at a church campout for teenage boys. The weather forecast called for thunderstorms with rain and strong winds throughout the day. That evening, I shared with the boys the story of how Jesus exercised dominion over the wind and the rain. While I was speaking, the wind continued to howl and the rain clouds came closer and closer. I said to the boys, "Everyone, stand to your feet. We are going to exercise our dominion over this storm, in Jesus' name!" The boys jumped up and we spoke to the wind and dark clouds, "Storm and wind, we command that you will not rain on our outdoor meeting. We command this in the mighty name of Jesus!" It never rained a drop on our entire campsite that evening nor during the night. The next day, the leaders of the campout shared with everyone that during the service, the storm came right up to our campsite and stopped. Our campsite was on the side of a lake. The leaders testified that they could see the rain falling on the lake the whole time I was preaching, yet it never came any closer! The storm remained stationary because we exercised our dominion in the name of Jesus. There is power in the mighty name of Jesus!

Hurricane Winds Destroyed

We have been given dominion over storms by using the name of Jesus, "You have made him to have dominion over the works of Your hands; You have put all things under his feet" (Psalm 8:6). If you are traveling around the world, you always want to make sure that you exercise your dominion in the name of Jesus. His name will work for you on foreign soil. The name of Jesus works in any language and in any nation of the world.

An evangelist friend of mine was ministering with his wife on the west coast of Mexico. While he was holding a crusade, a major hurricane developed into a category five storm with record 215-mile-per-hour sustained winds. The evangelist led the believers of that city to exercise their dominion and commanded the storm to be destroyed in the name of Jesus. They covered the city and the coast with the blood of Jesus and believed they would receive supernatural protection. Hurricane Patricia had no other choice but to fall apart when it hit the "Blood Line."

Living in South Florida can be intense during hurricane season. Over the years, we have seen the "Blood Line" prevent tropical storms and hurricanes from destroying our land. There is no power greater than the blood of Jesus. No named storm is greater than the name of Jesus. There is no other name in heaven, on the earth, or under the earth that can compete with the mighty name of Jesus! As a born-again believer, you have been given dominion to use the Word of God, the name of Jesus, and the blood of Jesus. You have been given dominion on this earth: "Fire and hail, snow and ice, hurricanes obeying his orders" (Psalm 148:8, MSG).

The disciples were amazed that the winds obeyed Jesus…but the winds will obey you when you exercise dominion in His name.

CHAPTER 10

ॐ

8TH KEY: YOU SHALL CALL UPON HIM

The eighth key to divine protection is found in Psalm 91, verse 15: "He shall call upon Me, and I will answer him; I will be with him in trouble; I will deliver him and honor him" (Psalm 91:15). Father God will respond when you call out for help and protection. The Lord will never snub you when you call. He doesn't hear you calling and say, "Oh no, it's him again," and then hit the reject button. The Lord will help you every time you call on Him for safety and protection.

Call Him First

When you call on the Lord, you'll never get a busy signal or a voicemail that says, "Hi. You have reached Jesus of Nazareth. Your call is important to me. I'm sorry I'm not at My throne at this time. If you would please leave your name, phone number, and a brief message, I'll return your call as soon as possible." Aren't you glad this will never happen?

When you call on the Lord, He will always answer: "'Call to Me, and I will answer you, and show you great and mighty things, which you do not know'" (Jeremiah 33:3). Calling on Jesus in a time of danger is the wisest thing you can possibly do. When you call on Him, He will answer you, He will be with you in trouble, He will deliver you, and He will honor you – every time (Psalm 91:14-15). Jesus does not watch as you go down in the sinking ship. He will answer you! He will deliver you! He will honor you!

How many times have you called the doctor's office when your child wasn't feeling well? How many times have you called a relative or friend when you needed help? Many times, God is the last person we call when we are in need of help. Don't let the Lord be the last one you call; let Him be the first one you call out to for help. But when you call on God, it must be done in faith. Notice that David called on the Lord in faith for help.

> *But know that the LORD has set apart for Himself him who is godly; the LORD will hear when I call to Him.*

> Psalm 4:3

> *In my distress I called upon the LORD, and cried out to my God; He heard my voice from His temple, and my cry came before Him, even to His ears.*

> Psalm 18:6

> *Because He has inclined His ear to me, therefore I will call upon Him as long as I live.*

> Psalm 116:2

Call Upon Him in Truth

When you call on Jesus, He will hear you and answer you with His supernatural power. The key to Him hearing your voice, however, is calling on Him in truth: "The LORD is near to all who call upon Him, to all who call upon Him in truth" (Psalm 145:18).

Does it really matter whether or not you call upon God in truth? If I have an emergency and dial 5-1-1, the voice on the other end will give me a traffic report, not dispatch emergency personnel to come to my aid. What is the problem? I dialed the wrong number. If I want to reach the emergency hotline, I must dial the correct number: 9-1-1.

If you cry, "God, why have You forsaken me," He will not answer the call. Why? You've dialed the wrong number. If you cry out, "God, why have You left me here to die," He will not answer that call, either. If you want to reach the Father, you must call upon Him in truth. You will never reach the Father by dialing up U-N-B-E-L-I-E-F. You must dial T-R-U-T-H, if you want to reach the Father's hotline. Jesus did not say He had the truth, He said He is the truth (John 14:6).

When you call upon the Lord in truth, you are calling based on His blood covenant promises. God is a blood covenant keeper to a thousand generations: "He remembers His covenant forever, the word which He commanded, for a thousand generations" (Psalm 105:8). He will never answer "No" to your call for help. He always answers "Yes" and "Amen" to all of His promises. The promises of God are always "Yes" when they are spoken by us through faith.

> *For all the promises of God in Him are Yes, and in Him Amen, to the glory of God through us.*

> 2 Corinthians 1:20

Torrential Rain Stopped Instantaneously

When you call on the Lord, you may only have time to say, "Jesus!" You may only have a split second, only time for you to say, "The blood!" This happened to me once while driving on the highway in heavy rain. My wife and I were on our way to church on a Wednesday night. We were driving on I-95 in Miami and it was dark with torrential rain falling. In South Florida, there is rain and there is *torrential rain*. The each drop seemed bucket sized. The wind was so strong that our windshield wipers could not handle it and suddenly stopped working.

Driving on the highway that night in a torrential downpour with broken windshield wipers, I only had a split second to say something. If I had been meditating on negative thoughts , then that is what would have come out of my mouth. I would have spoken words according to what was overflowing in my heart. If you face danger and a four letter word comes out of your mouth (*"Oh...bleep!"*), then you know you are full of another four letter word...fear! If your heart is filled with fear, then your mouth will use offensive words to express what overflows in your heart. You must sanctify your heart and your mouth with the washing of water by the Word (Ephesians 5:26).

The rains covered the windshield and I was completely blinded to what was in front of us on the highway because I had no working wipers. With time for only one cry, I shouted "THE BLOOD!" In that very instant, the rain immediately stopped! I don't mean it slowed down to a light sprinkle. The rain completely stopped. When I called on the blood of Jesus, the winds and rain obeyed.

Some may say that was just a coincidence. Those people do not believe in the supernatural power of the name and the blood of Jesus. They think that such methods are for weird religious fanatics who believe in magical, mystical and spooky powers. No my friend, the name of Jesus is not magical, and the blood of Jesus is not mystical. They are mighty and they are powerful! The name of Jesus, the blood of Jesus, and the Word of God are what connect you to the supernatural. When you call upon the Lord in truth, He will answer you with His supernatural protection every time!

> *The name of the LORD is a strong tower; the righteous run to it and are safe.*

Proverbs 18:10

Abba, Daddy

If you are a parent, you are familiar with hearing in the middle of the night, "Daddy" or "Mommy." No matter if you are fast asleep, when your little one cries out your name, you come to the rescue. Your heavenly Father wants you to call on Him. This honors Him. If my children are in danger, I expect them to call on my help. How much more does our heavenly Father expect us to call on Him?

There is nothing more hurtful than to know your own child does not trust in your protection. If your child were to say to you, "The reason I didn't call on you is because I know you probably wouldn't have done anything," how would that make you feel? Failure to call on the Father for help when trouble arises is an indication of a lack of trust. When you are in danger, Father God expects you to call on Him first.

> *For you did not receive the spirit of bondage again to fear, but you received the Spirit of adoption by whom we cry out, "Abba, Father."*

Romans 8:15

The Aramaic word for father is *Abba*.[29] When you call on your heavenly Father for help, it brings Him honor. When you call on Him, He will answer you. When you honor Him, He will honor you: "I will set him on high, because he has known My name. He shall call upon Me, and I will answer him; I will be with him in trouble; I will deliver him and honor him" (Psalm 91:14-15).

Calling Him at the Shopping Mall

Don't ever think that God is too busy to help you. And don't think of yourself as insignificant, either. You are loved by God and hated by the devil. Don't think for a moment that the devil will leave you alone. Satan is always seeking whom he may devour (1 Peter 5:8). Every day, he is on the attack. A car accident is not an accident in the devil's eyes. He times his attacks to accomplish as much stealing, killing, and destroying as possible. You have been redeemed from destruction by the precious blood of Christ (1 Peter 1:18-19). Don't leave home without first covering yourself and your family with the blood.

I know of a young Christian lady who had taken her friend to go shopping in a mall. When they got out of their car in the dark parking lot, they were approached by two men. Feeling very uneasy, the Christian lady covered herself, her friend, and her car with the blood of Jesus and prayed for the Lord's protection. When the women came back to their car to leave, the two men were still there. The men stood and laughed as the young lady attempted to start her car with no success. She cried out, "The blood of Jesus," and commanded the car to start in Jesus' name. On the next attempt, the car started. As she pulled out of the parking lot, she noticed that both men looked stunned. When she returned home, she told her father what had happened. He checked to see if something was wrong with the new car battery he had recently installed. When he opened up the hood, he discovered the car battery was missing!

God knows how to start your car without a battery! When you need help from the Lord, all you have to do is call on Jesus. There is power in His Word, His name, and His blood. The Lord is ready to gather you underneath His wings. Just call on Him and He will rescue you every time!

CHAPTER 11

PERMANENCY OF LIFE

Permanency of life is promised at the end of Psalm 91: "With long life I will satisfy him, and show him My salvation" (Psalm 91:16). The Hebrew word translated "salvation" here is *yeshuwah*, which means, "saved, deliverance, victory, prosperity, health, help, salvation, save, saving, welfare." [30] The name "Jesus" comes from this Hebrew word, yeshuwah. The last promise of Psalm 91 tells us that when we make Yahweh our place of refuge, God will reveal Himself as "Yahweh is salvation" or "Yahweh is the one who protects."

What Does God Consider to be "Long Life"?

Adam and Eve's third son was named Seth. The son of Seth was Enosh. It was during the days of Enosh that men began to call upon the Lord: "And as for Seth, to him also a son was born; and he named him Enosh. Then men began to call on the name of the LORD" (Genesis 4:26).

During this time, men lived for many years. Adam lived for 930 years. Seth lived for 920 years. Enosh lived 905 years.

Enoch, the great-grandfather of Noah, walked with God for 365 years before God took him to heaven (Genesis 5:23-24). Methuselah, Noah's grandfather, lived 969 years. When men walked and talked with God, they lived so long that it seemed like they would never die. When you make the Lord your place of dwelling, you, too, will enjoy long life.

> *Hear, my son, and receive my sayings, and the years of your life will be many.*

Proverbs 4:10

What would you consider to be a "long life"? Is reaching seventy years of age a long life? Eighty? The vast majority of Christians do not live what the Bible considers a long life. According to God's Word, He has given us one hundred and twenty years of life: "His days shall be one hundred and twenty years" (Genesis 6:3). You may be thinking, "This is too extreme! There is hardly anyone who lives to be one hundred years old!" Yes, it sounds extraordinary, because it is not natural but supernatural. When you live a long life according to God's promise, it will be a sign and wonder to others. They will look at you and not believe how good you look for your age. Why? Because you live under the shadow of the Almighty. You dwell in the secret place of the Most High.

You may have always considered it rare for a person to live to be one hundred years old, but this should not be the case. God has gifted us with the ability to live a long life. You may be thinking, "There is no way I want to live to be a hundred years old. If I live to be that old, I'll probably be crippled with arthritis, half blind, and won't even know my own phone number!" That is the very reason why you need to present your body to God and have your mind renewed with His Word (Romans 12:2). You have to believe that it is God's will for you to have a long life and remain strong, healthy, and wise.

70 to 80 Years Is Not "Long Life"

The prayer of Moses in Psalm 90:12 states, "So teach us to number our days, that we may gain a heart of wisdom." Moses knew Israel had angered the Lord when they refused to make Him their dwelling place (Psalm 90:3-7). As a result, the Hebrew children were promised only seventy years of life or at the most, possibly eighty years: "You have set our iniquities before You, our secret sins in the light of Your countenance. For all our days have passed away in Your wrath; we finish our years like a sigh. The days of our lives are seventy years; and if by reason of strength they are eighty years" (Psalm 90:8-10).

Psalm 90 speaks to a man who lives in his own strength, saying his days are limited to seventy or eighty years. But the writer of Psalm 91 communicates the Lord's promise of longevity given to the one who does make the Lord his dwelling place: "With long life I will satisfy him, and show him My salvation" (Psalm 91:16). Those who make the Lord their refuge can be guaranteed a long life of satisfaction, not sorrow.

Age seventy or eighty may seem old by our society's standards, but not according to God's standards. Caleb stated that he was strong and was ready to enlist in the Israelite army at age eighty-five. He was ready to take on a whole mountain of giants because the Lord had kept him alive and was his strength: "And now, behold, the LORD has kept me alive, as He said, these forty-five years, ever since the LORD spoke this word to Moses while Israel wandered in the wilderness; and now, here I am this day, eighty-five years old. As yet I am as strong this day as on the day that Moses sent me; just as my strength was then, so now is my strength for war, both for going out and for coming in. Now therefore, give me this mountain" (Joshua 14:10-12).

Length of Days

The Lord commanded Israel to remember their blood covenant with Him so their days would be prolonged (Deuteronomy 4:26; 6:2-3). If Israel made the decision to keep His statutes, they would live long on the earth and prosper: "You shall therefore keep His statutes and His commandments which I commanded you today, that it may go well with you and with your children after you, and that you may prolong your days in the land which the LORD your God is giving you for all time" (Deuteronomy 4:40).

When the Bible talks about "prolonging your days" or having "length of days," it is referring to living a long life: "The fear of the LORD prolongs days, but the years of the wicked will be shortened" (Proverbs 10:27). Remember, God's standard of long life is 120 years, not 70 years or 80 years (Genesis 6:3).

Moses lived a life in the presence of God and as a result, God prolonged his life to 120 years. At the end of his life, Moses was not weak and bent over with crippling arthritis. He was not senile and unable to think straight. He was strong, healthy and had no need for reading glasses: "Moses was one hundred and twenty years old when he died. His eyes were not dim nor his natural vigor diminished" (Deuteronomy 34:7).

There are other scriptures that promise longevity. David spoke of how his request for life was granted with length of days: "He asked life from You, and You gave it to him — Length of days forever and ever" (Psalm 21:4). The wisdom of God promises, "Length of days is in her right hand; in her left hand are riches and honor" (Proverbs 3:16). The Apostle Paul quoted the Torah, instructing children to honor their parents in the Lord and receive the promise of longevity: "Children, obey your parents in the Lord, for this is right. 'Honor your father and mother' which is the first commandment with promise, 'that it may be well with you and you may live long on the earth'" (Ephesians 6:1-3).

120 Years of Life

Remember, when Noah found grace, he lived 950 years (Genesis 6:8; 9:29). But during the time of Noah, God saw the wickedness of man and reduced his longevity: "And the LORD said, 'My Spirit shall not strive with man forever, for he is indeed flesh; yet his days shall be one hundred and twenty years'" (Genesis 6:3). The *New Living Translation* of this verse reads this way, "In the future, their normal lifespan will be no more than 120 years."

After this judgment of God, the longevity of man began to be reduced. Abraham's wife, Sarah, lived 127 years (Genesis 23:1). Abraham lived 175 years: "Then Abraham breathed his last and died in a good old age, an old man and full of years, and was gathered to his people" (Genesis 25:8). Isaac lived 180 years: "Now the days of Isaac were one hundred and eighty years. So Isaac breathed his last and died, and was gathered to his people, being old and full of days. And his sons Esau and Jacob buried him" (Genesis 35:28-29). David was said to have lived a long life that was full of days: "So when David was old and full of days, he made his son Solomon king over Israel" (1 Chronicles 23:1). "So he died in a good old age, full of days and riches and honor" (1 Chronicles 29:28).

The scripture does not tell how old Anna the prophetess was when she met Jesus as he was being dedicated in the temple (Luke 2:38), however, it does specify that Anna was a woman of a great age; "Now there was one, Anna, a prophetess...She was of a great age" (Luke 2:36). We know she was a widow for 84 years, after she had lived with her husband for seven years from her virginity (Luke 2:36-37). This would mean she was well over 100 years old, serving in the temple day and night.

> *You must serve only the LORD your God. If you do, I will bless you with food and water, and I will protect you from illness. There will be no miscarriages or infertility in your land, and I will give you long, full lives.*

> Exodus 23:25-26, NLT

> *For You meet him with the blessings of goodness; You set a crown of pure gold upon his head. He asked life from You, and You gave it to him—length of days forever and ever.*

> Psalm 21:3-4

The Lord wants you to enjoy a long life, experiencing His blessings and goodness. If you are not enjoying the abundance of God at its best, there is still time! Have you celebrated your 100th birthday yet? Then why think it's too late? God wants you to possess the good land and enjoy it for many years. He wants you to be like Job who carried around his grandkids, great grandkids, and his great-great grandkids: "After this Job lived one hundred and forty years, and saw his children and grandchildren for four generations" (Job 42:16). So don't give up! You're young and have a bright future ahead of you. Don't let the devil talk you out of living a long life to its fullest and best. Take freely what belongs to you as you walk with God and enjoy His goodness.

> *You shall walk in all the ways which the LORD your God has commanded you, that you may live and that it may be well with you, and that you may prolong your days in the land which you shall possess.*

> Deuteronomy 5:33

Are You Satisfied with Long Life?

I was born in 1967, just before the prophetic event of the Six Day War in Israel. I was born at a miraculous time, just before events that prophesied of the coming of the Messiah in my generation (Matthew 24:32-34; Luke 21:24). I don't want to die. I want to live to be a part of the *harpazo*, which is a Greek word for the great catching away [31] mentioned in 1 Thessalonians 4:17.

Is that your attitude? Do you want to live to see prophetic events realized, or are you satisfied already? Your desire has a lot to do with your longevity on this earth. If you are satisfied and ready to move on to the other side, then that probably will happen sooner than you think. But for those of us who are not satisfied, we can believe for up to 100 years, plus. We have God's Word on it. He has promised 120 years of life on this earth to those who make Him their refuge.

My father-in-law was raised in Lebanon. Till this day, he talks about the awesomeness of the cedar trees of Lebanon. You are righteous in Christ Jesus and are to flourish with longevity like the cedar trees of Lebanon that are planted into good ground.

> *The [uncompromisingly] righteous shall flourish like the palm tree [be long-lived, stately, upright, useful, and fruitful]; they shall grow like a cedar in Lebanon [majestic, stable, durable, and incorruptible].*

Psalm 92:12 AMPC

We are to thrive like cedar trees in Lebanon. We are to flourish like the palm trees in the Caribbean. We are to be like trees that bend but do not break. When the winds of adversity come with all their fury, we simply bend and remain stable. We are to prosper and never stop growing in life and wisdom as we age. The Lord has provided a blood covenant to give us a long, satisfied life, filled with good things as our youth is renewed like the eagle's: "Who satisfies your mouth with good things, so that your youth is renewed like the eagle's" (Psalm 103:5).

*Any weapon that is formed
against you is powerless
when you are dwelling in the
secret place of protection.*

CHAPTER 12

 CS

HE WILL DELIVER US

Let's look at a familiar passage in the Bible that illustrates how the Lord will protect His people from any threat of danger. King Nebuchadnezzar made an image of gold about 90 feet tall that was to be used for both political and religious purposes. He made the image of gold to institute a new religious worship that would help unify the Babylonian government with the Hebrew people. The Jewish companions of Daniel living in Babylonian captivity with him were Hananiah, whose Hebrew name means "the Lord is gracious," [32] Mishael, whose Hebrew name means "who is God's," [33] and Azariah, whose Hebrew name means "whom God aids." [34] The three Hebrew names of these young men give us a picture of divine protection - The Lord is gracious; He is with us; and He is our help in times of danger.

Even though the king had given these three men Babylonian names - Shadrach, Meshach, and Abed-Nego - they rejected a Babylonian identity. They refused to follow the king's decree to bow and worship the golden image (Daniel 3:12). The king warned the three Hebrew men that if they did not fall down and worship the image, they would be immediately cast into a burning fiery furnace. The capital punishment of burning someone alive was a common practice in Babylon.

When the three Hebrew men heard the consequences for failing to bow, they responded, "O Nebuchadnezzar, we have no need to answer you in this matter" (Daniel 3:16). During this time, Nebuchadnezzar was the highest in command on earth. Can you imagine responding to the highest in command this way? Visualize yourself surrounded by the most violent and powerful terrorist group on the earth. The leader of this group has forced you to stand in front of a camera to broadcast your image around the world on a live webcast. The terrorist leader is raging mad and has his knife at your throat. In his fury, he shouts, "Is it true, that you refuse to renounce your faith in Jesus Christ?" You then point your finger between the leader's eyes and fearlessly declare, "I have no need to answer you in this matter. My God will deliver me!" That is what a courageous blood warrior would do. You do not have to cower in fear, even in the face of death.

The three Hebrew men's confidence was based in their knowledge of the Lord's power of deliverance. They would have been familiar with how the Lord delivered Moses and Israel from Pharaoh and the Egyptians. They would have known the promises of divine protection the Lord gave His people: "When you pass through the waters, I will be with you; and through the rivers, they shall not overflow you. When you walk through the fire, you shall not be burned, nor shall the flame scorch you" (Isaiah 43:2). They believed the same God who delivered Israel out of Egypt would also deliver them from the Babylonian king.

Who Will Deliver You?

When Nebuchadnezzar said, "And who is the god who will deliver you from my hands?" (Daniel 3:15), the three Hebrew men confidently responded, "Our God whom we serve is able to deliver us from the burning fiery furnace, and **He will deliver us** from your hand, O king" (Daniel 3:17, emphasis mine). Not one of them wavered, but all three agreed that the Lord would deliver them from the hand of the king. How could these men have such unshakable faith unless they already knew the promises of God's protection? They didn't say something politically correct like, "O king, we're sorry we offended you and violated your law." No, they stood up for what they believed. They had complete confidence that the Lord would deliver them from death. How could they be so confident of the Lord's deliverance? They had already meditated in the promises of His protection.

> *But the salvation of the righteous is from the LORD; He is their strength in the time of trouble. And the LORD shall help them and deliver them; He shall deliver them from the wicked, and save them, because they trust in Him.*

Psalm 37:39-40

Hananiah, Mishael, and Azariah had full assurance of the Lord's deliverance but informed the king that even if they had no promise of deliverance, they still would not bow to his false god: "But if not, let it be known to you, O king, that we do not serve your gods, nor will we worship the gold image which you have set up" (Daniel 3:18). Their refusal to bow and worship a false god was based in their decision to obey God's commandment to not go after other gods to serve them (Deuteronomy 6:13-14). But all three Hebrew men agreed that God would deliver them. They were in one accord in their faith, which shows that they all had a revelation of divine protection prior to this event.

The king was outraged at the audacity of these Hebrew men. In his fury, he gave orders to heat the furnace seven times hotter than before. I mean really, how hot can you make a furnace? Fire is fire, right? So why did the king say this? It was to create fear in the hearts of these three men. A terrorist always uses fear as their ultimate weapon. They attempt to cripple their victim with fear by making vicious and horrible threats. They intimidate by saying words like, "Either you renounce Christ, or we will torture and kill both you and your entire family!" But when you know that the Lord is your refuge and His angels are encamped around you, you just point your finger at their nose and declare, "In the name of Jesus, you cannot kill or injure any one of us! We are covered by the blood of Jesus and His angels are encamped around us. If anyone should be pleading for mercy, it should be you!"

The Fire Had No Power

When Nebuchadnezzar had the three Hebrew men cast into the burning furnace, his own men died from the heat, but the three Hebrew men were protected from both the heat of the burning flames and from inhaling the smoke. The king was astonished when he saw the three men walking around the blazing furnace. Then all of a sudden, Nebuchadnezzar saw a fourth man in the furnace whom he described as "like the Son of God" (Daniel 3:25). The Angel of God had been sent to encamp and deliver the three Hebrew men from the furnace.

The king and his administrators examined the three men after they came out of the furnace and testified that their hair was not singed, their garments were not affected, nor did they even smell like smoke (Daniel 3:27). Isn't that awesome! The fire had no power on their body!

I remember one time I ministered healing to a teenage boy who had just had his arm severely burned from boiling water. I went to his apartment to pray for him and when I saw his arm, I could tell that part of the outer skin had been completely burned off. I asked him on a scale of 1 to 10 how bad the pain was. He answered, "Zero!" His mom testified to me that even though her son's arm looked really bad, he had no pain. I asked her if he was taking any pain medication, but she said he never needed any. They just covered his arm with the blood of Jesus and he experienced no pain. There is power in the blood of Jesus!

Any weapon that is formed against you is powerless when you are dwelling in the secret place of protection. Jesus assured us that our heavenly Father, who takes care of the grass of the field that is later thrown into the oven, would completely protect His children from anything that would try to harm us – even protecting the very hair on our heads (Matthew 6:30; 10:30). That's our mighty God!

Just imagine the look on a terrorist's face when his bullets have no power against a blood warrior, when his threatening words are ignored and cause no fear. A terrorist is completely helpless when he comes face to face with a believer who knows he is in blood covenant with Almighty God. That believer is fearless because he has the assurance that he is surrounded by the angelic army of heaven.

When Nebuchadnezzar had the three Hebrew men taken out of the furnace, he began to praise the Lord by saying, "Blessed be the God of Shadrach, Meshach, and Abed-Nego, who sent His Angel and delivered His servants who trusted in Him" (Daniel 3:28). The king recognized that the Hebrew's verbal declaration of their confidence in the Lord's deliverance is what sent the Angel of God to protect them from harm.

King Nebuchadnezzar made a decree that no one could speak against the God of Shardrach, Meshach, and Abed-Nego because, "there is no other God who can deliver like this" (Daniel 3:29). Isn't that so true? There is no one like our Father God! He will send His angels to save you when you make Him your place of refuge (Exodus 23:20).

Hananiah, Mishael, and Azariah are examples of how faith in the blood covenant really works. These Hebrew men stood on the blood covenant promises of preservation and overcame persecution. The enemy endeavored to exterminate them, but they remained unharmed. Even in the face of great persecution and perilous times, God's covenant people will be kept safe because they know their blood covenant of supernatural protection.

We must be quick to pray for someone and slow to speak, not slow to pray and quick to give our advice.

CHAPTER 13

∞

HEDGE OF PROTECTION

Over the years, people have correlated tragedies in their personal lives to what happened in the life of Job. They relate to how Job suffered and like Job, they choose to bless God rather than curse Him. Job blessed the Lord for something tragic that happened to both him and his household: "The LORD gave, and the LORD has taken away; Blessed be the name of the LORD" (Job 1:21). The Hebrew word for "blessed" is *barak*, which means, "to kneel, bless, be blessed." [35] But Job unknowingly blessed the Lord for something Satan was behind.

When it comes to our lives, our health, our family, the Lord is the giver and not the taker. The only things God takes away from us are those things that are under the curse of sin. I like to keep it as simple as possible:

GOD is GOOD

the DEVIL is EVIL

If it's good, then it's from God. If it's evil, then it's from the devil. Jesus came to give us life and to take away our sins, sickness, and anything that is under the curse. He did not come to take away children from their parents or to take away good health and replace it with sickness and disease.

God is the giver of blessings, not the taker of blessings. God is in the business of giving life, and Satan is in the business of taking away life (John 10:10). Job gave the Lord credit for giving and taking away the life of his children and giving and taking away his health. The Lord gave Job good health. The Lord's angels hedged Jobs' entire family from Satan. The hedge of protection was not keeping Job safe from God. When you understand what truly happened to Job and his family, it will help you avoid tragedy and remain safely in the hedge of the Lord's protection.

When God asked Satan if he had considered the excellence of His servant Job, Satan answered that he noticed God had placed a hedge of protection around Job and his family: "Have You not made a hedge around him, around his household, and around all that he has on every side? You have blessed the work of his hands, and his possessions have increased in the land" (Job 1:10). The Hebrew word for "hedge" is *suwk*, which means "to entwine, to shut in, to fence, to hedge up." [36] Even though Satan had his eyes on Job and his family, he was unable to break down the hedge of protection. So what eventually caused the hedge of protection to be breeched? You may have always heard that it was God who let down the hedge. Let's first establish that God does not permit or allow the wicked one to trespass the hedge of protection.

Blessing God for Evil

Job was a God-fearing man who made ten burnt offerings every morning according to the number of his children (Job 1:2, 5). He did this out of fear that his children may have blessed God in an evil manner with sin in their hearts.

> *So it was, when the days of feasting had run their course, that Job would send and sanctify them, and he would rise early in the morning and offer burnt offerings according to*

the number of them all. For Job said, "It may be that my sons have sinned and cursed God in their hearts." Thus Job did regularly.

Job 1:5

Remember that the Hebrew word for "blessed" is barak. Interestingly, this same Hebrew word, barak, is translated "cursed" in Job 1:5: "For Job said, 'It may be that my sons have sinned and cursed (*barak*) God in their hearts.' Thus Job did regularly" (explanation mine). The Hebrew word normally translated "curse" or "cursed" is *naqab*, as used in Job 3:1: "After this Job opened his mouth and cursed (*naqab*) the day of his birth" (explanation mine). But in this instance in the book of Job, barak is used to speak of blessing the Lord in an evil manner. [37] Four times in the book of Job, the verb barak is translated "curse" or "cursed" (Job 1:5; 1:11; 2:5; 2:9).

When Job unknowingly blessed the Lord for doing evil, God did not account it to him as sin or blaming God with wrong (Job 1:22). However, when you bless the Lord as both giving and taking away what is good in your life, you are blaming God with wrong. You are blessing the Lord in an evil manner and not worshiping Him in spirit and in truth (John 4:24). We are not to bless the Lord as the One who takes from us; we are to bless Him as the One who gives us richly all things to enjoy (1 Timothy 6:17).

You may have been mad at yourself, mad at circumstances, or mad at people who have done you wrong, but you should never be mad at God. You should never shake your fist at Him in blame. Be sure of this fact, your Father has never and will never allow anyone or anything evil to hurt you or your family. You never have to bless God for being the One who makes you suffer. He is not behind the evil. When you understand your Father in the new covenant perspective, in the light of Jesus Christ, you will never be angry or offended at Him. You will know Him as the one who gives life more abundantly. It's the devil who comes to steal, kill, and destroy (John 10:10).

The Thing I Greatly Feared

Job made ten burnt offerings every morning for his children because he was moved in fear that one day they might possibly suffer or even die because of their sins. The fear Job had of losing his children was expressed after they were all killed, "For the thing I greatly feared has come upon me, and what I dreaded has happened to me. I am not at ease, nor am I quiet; I have no rest, for trouble comes" (Job 3:25-26).

Job expressed his dread of God, even though He had protected Job and his family in the past, "Therefore I am terrified at His presence; when I consider this, I am afraid of Him. For God made my heart weak, and the Almighty terrifies me" (Job 23:15-16). To properly fear the Lord is not to be terrified of Him but to worship and reverence Him. You should have complete confidence in the Lord's protection. You never want to tell your kids, "I'm scared to death that you're one day going to get yourself hurt or even killed." These are not words of life but words of death spoken over your children. Death and life cannot mix together in your mouth. Do not mix death and life words in your prayers, such as, "Father God, please keep me safe as I go to sleep. And if I should die before I awake, I pray the Lord my soul to take." Only speak words of life to yourself and to your family. Speak words of death to the enemy, enemies such as sickness or disease.

What Is God Doing?

Job's account shows us what it was like to have limited knowledge of God's nature prior to the teachings of the Torah. Many commentators agree that Job lived prior to Abraham. That would mean that Job had no written Bible, no prophet or teacher who could shed some light. He had no pastor or local church. He had no knowledge or understanding of Satan, devils, demons, or spiritual warfare. He just simply believed that God was behind all his tragedy. He talked with God like Noah and Enoch did and received council, but Job lacked understanding of the ways of the blood covenant-keeping God. "Oh that I were as in months past, as in the days when God watched over me" (Job 29:2).

Job acknowledged that he uttered things about God he did not understand. "Then Job answered the LORD and said: 'I know that You can do everything, and that no purpose of Yours can be withheld from You. You asked, "Who is this who hides counsel without knowledge?" Therefore I have uttered what I did not understand, things too wonderful for me, which I did not know'" (Job 42:1-3). We cannot relate to Job in the area of ignorance. We have the Bible and the Holy Spirit who lives in us. We have been blessed in these last days with the increase of knowledge and understanding from apostles, prophets, evangelists, pastors and teachers (Ephesians 4:11).

Job found it difficult to plead his case before God since he had no mediator, "For He is not a man, as I am, that I may answer Him, and that we should go to court together. Nor is there any mediator between us, who may lay his hand on us both. Let Him take His rod away from me, and do not let dread of Him terrify me. Then I would speak and not fear Him, but it is not so with me" (Job 9:32-35). Job was terrified of not having an arbitrator to stand between him and the God who held a rod. This is not the case for you and me. We have Jesus, who is our mediator of the new covenant (Hebrews 12:24). No longer can the devil just waltz up to God and charge us with sin. We have our mediator, King Jesus, who is seated at the right hand of God interceding for and defending us. God is not mad at you. He does not sit on His throne holding a rod ready to strike you and your family for whatever reason.

Job regarded God as hard to figure out and the one behind death, "He does great things past finding out, yes, wonders without number. If He goes by me, I do not see Him; if He moves past, I do not perceive Him; if He takes away, who can hinder Him? Who can say to Him, 'What are You doing'" (Job 9:10-12). Have you ever heard someone say when facing a premature death situation, "God decided to take him/her"? When something tragic happens, the first one to be blamed is usually God. "Hey God!

Why did You allow this? What are You doing?" This should not be the case. Jesus revealed to us the nature and character of the loving Father who wants only good for His children. Jesus prayed that we would know the Father loves us just as much as He loves His Son Jesus: "And that the world may know that You have sent Me, and have loved them as You have loved Me" (John 17:23).

We should be aware of the blood covenant God has made with the seed of Abraham. We are to enjoy a long life of protection, health, and peace. You may have friends like Job who have tried to provide you with answers during a time of crisis. Job's friends were sincere, but they were sincerely wrong.

Friendly Wrong Advice

Have you ever noticed how people like to give you their advice? We all have a tendency to like to tell people why, when, how, and what they need to do. This is especially true when we see our brother or sister suffering. We may feel like we have all the answers. We think, "If only he had listened to me, this would have never happened." We must be quick to pray for someone and slow to speak, not slow to pray and quick to give our advice. You may be sincere in your motives, but your advice could be sincerely wrong.

Sometimes the only thing that needs to be said is, "I am always here for you. I am praying for you and you're going to make it through to the other side!" It is amazing how those simple words of hope, when spoken from a loving and sincere heart, will bring encouragement to someone who has gone through tremendous suffering. Just letting that person know you are there if they ever need you can truly bring comfort to the brokenhearted.

Job was surrounded by friends who wanted to give him some "friendly advice." Job's friends were convinced they had all the answers and that he just needed to listen and learn. His friend, Bildad, concluded that Job's sons and daughters were killed by God due to their own sin: "If your sons have sinned against Him, He has cast them away for their transgression" (Job 8:4).

Job's other friend, Eliphaz, concluded that Job's tragedy was a result of the chastening of God: "Behold, happy is the man whom God corrects; therefore do not despise the chastening of the Almighty" (Job 5:17). Eliphaz reassured Job that God is the one who bruises and wounds, but in the end, He would keep Job and his family safe from future destruction: "For He bruises, but He binds up; He wounds, but His hands make whole. He shall deliver you in six troubles, yes, in seven no evil shall touch you" (Job 5:18-19).

But Job knew something was missing. "Why would God watch over me and my family all these years and suddenly decide to strike us down?" Job knew there was something wrong with the picture his friends were painting for him.

Jesus gave us an accurate picture of our loving heavenly Father. When you want to know about your heavenly Father, always go to Jesus, "I am the good shepherd; and I know My sheep, and am known by My own. As the Father knows Me, even so I know the Father; and I lay down My life for the sheep" (John 10:14-15).

Ultimately God restored Job, giving him ten more children: three beautiful daughters and seven sons (Job 42:13-15). The closing verses of Job show that the hedge of protection around Job and his family was never again broken down.

> *And the Lord turned the captivity of Job and restored his fortunes, when he prayed for his friends; also the Lord gave Job twice as much as he had before…After this, Job lived 140 years, and saw his sons and his sons' sons, even to four generations. So Job died, an old man and full of days.*

> Job 42:10, 16-17; AMPC

The Book of the Blood Covenant

In Psalm 91:4, it says that you will be surrounded by the Lord's shield: "His truth shall be your shield and buckler." The shield and buckler encircles all around you and your family as a hedge of protection. The Lord promised a hedge of angelic protection for Israel in the wilderness: "Behold, I send an Angel before you to keep you in the way and to bring you into the place which I have prepared" (Exodus 23:20). The Hebrew word for "keep" in this verse is *shamar*, which means: "to hedge about, guard, to protect, attend, to keep, preserve, reserve, save, watch." [38]

After the Lord declared these promises of protection, Moses wrote all the words the Lord had spoken and read them to Israel. This book was called, "The Book of the Covenant" (Exodus 24:7), and it included the promises the Lord made to take sickness from their midst (Exodus 23:25) and provide angelic protection (Exodus 23:20). After Moses read from "The Book of the Covenant," he made a blood sacrifice on the altar, sprinkling half of the blood on the altar and half of the blood on the people.

> *And Moses took half the blood and put it in basins, and half the blood he sprinkled on the altar. Then he took the Book of the Covenant and read in the hearing of the people. And they said, "All that the LORD has said we will do, and be obedient." And Moses took the blood, sprinkled it on the people, and said, "This is the blood of the covenant which the LORD has made with you according to all these words."*

Exodus 24:6-8

The Bible is our Book of the Blood Covenant. Jesus Christ shed His blood and presented it before Father God (Hebrews 9:23-24). When you see any promise in God's Word, know that it is bought and paid for by the precious blood of the Lamb of God. You have a blood covenant with God and you have been given His Blood Covenant Book.

The act of someone "pleading the blood of Jesus" or "sprinkling the blood of Jesus" on someone or something for divine protection is connected to this act of Moses: "For when Moses had spoken every precept to all the people according to the law, he took the blood of calves and goats, with water, scarlet wool, and hyssop, and sprinkled both the book itself and all the people, saying, 'This is the blood of the covenant which God has commanded you'" (Hebrews 9:19-20).

Notice that Moses sprinkled the blood on both the book and on the people of Israel and declared, "This is the blood of the covenant which the LORD has made with you according to all these words" (Exodus 24:8). The Lord has given you His Blood Covenant Book. Don't just carry a Bible; let the Bible carry you. Let the Word of God be the final authority in every area of your life.

As far as safety is concerned, God has made a blood covenant with you and your family that He will keep you hedged inside His protection. His Word promises it. His blood has purchased it. All you have to do is believe, receive and act in faith on the blood covenant.

Hedge Around You and Your Family

When the Lord instructed the priests to bless the children of Israel, He instructed them to say, "The LORD bless you and keep you" (Numbers 6:24). This is the same Hebrew word *shamar* mentioned in Exodus 23:20, "Behold, I send an Angel before you to keep you in the way." Here, shamar means "to keep, to hedge about, guard, to protect." [39] This means that when the priests pronounced the blessing on the children of Israel, they placed a divine hedge of protection around them.

The entire priestly blessing is found in Numbers 6:22-26.

And the LORD spoke to Moses, saying: "Speak to Aaron and his sons, saying, 'This is the way you shall bless the children of Israel. Say to them: "The Lord bless you and keep you; the Lord make His face shine upon you, and be gracious to you; the Lord lift up His countenance upon you, and give you peace." '"

Do you remember the Hebrew word for peace? If you said shalom, you are correct. Again, shalom means "welfare, health, prosperity, peace, rest, safety, all is well, wholeness." [40] The blessing over the children of Israel included a hedge of protection that ensured their safety, welfare, rest, and peace. The blessing of shalom over Israel covered everything they needed for a good and blessed life.

Every day, you can apply the blood of Jesus and keep the hedge of protection over you and your family. You do not have to live in fear of something tragic happening to your children as they drive on the highway, go to school or to the mall. You can live at peace knowing the hedge of protection is preserved by faith. You don't have to wonder like Job did, "Is my child going to die because they may have sinned?" That fear cannot be tolerated. If God would keep Rahab the harlot and her heathen family safe, then surely He will keep you and your family safe from harm (Joshua 2:17-21). God is merciful and full of compassion. Your heavenly Father has given you dominion to keep the hedge of protection over you and your family.

CHAPTER 14

CS

THE VOICE OF WISDOM

To him the doorkeeper opens, and the sheep hear his voice;
and he calls his own sheep by name and leads them out.
And when he brings out his own sheep, he goes before
them; and the sheep follow him, for they know his voice.

John 10:3-4

Wherever you go, it is imperative that you are sensitive to the voice of the Spirit. That means you are listening inside. Remember, the Greater One lives inside of you (1 John 4:4). Jesus said He would send us the Holy Spirit, who would lead and guide us into all truth: "However, when He, the Spirit of truth, has come, He will guide you into all truth; for He will not speak on His own authority, but whatever He hears He will speak; and He will tell you things to come" (John 16:13).

The primary way the Lord communicates to us is through our spirit, the inward man (2 Corinthians 4:16; 1 Peter 3:4). Most commonly, you will hear His voice inside your spirit and not an audible voice from heaven.

> *For as many as are led by the Spirit of God, these are sons of God.*

Romans 8:14

> *The Spirit Himself bears witness with our spirit that we are children of God.*

Romans 8:16

> *For You will light my lamp; the LORD my God will enlighten my darkness.*

Psalm 18:28

> *The spirit of a man is the lamp of the LORD, searching all the inner depths of his heart.*

Proverbs 20:27

When you listen to the voice of the Spirit, you are following the voice of wisdom. The Holy Spirit will always lead you in the right direction. He will never lead you into a situation where you will be injured or impaired. He will always lead you out of harm's way. When you hear His voice, you must follow His voice. For example, you may sense a voice inside telling you, "You need to slow down," and as you do, suddenly the car in front of you slams on their brakes. What happened? The Holy Spirit alerted you of things to come. He has your protection in mind, but you need to be in tune to His voice. The more you get to know His Word and fellowship with Him in prayer, the more you will recognize His leading. When you cover yourself with the blood of Jesus and speak the blessing of the Lord's divine protection, the divine blessing of shalom will surround you.

Divine Protection when Led by the Spirit

Here is a question I would like for you to think on for a moment before you answer:

If one day, you and your family decided you would travel all over the world telling people about Jesus, would you and your family receive the same protection the Apostle Paul did?

Now before you answer the question, read it again slowly. Make sure you are looking for key words that will give you the correct answer.

If your answer was "no" or "not necessarily," then you are correct. If you answered "Yes," you may be saying, "What! How could you say such a thing? That's unbelief!" Hold on and don't get upset. Let me explain. To dwell in the shelter of the Lord's protection, you have to be following His lead. Notice that in the question, it says "*you decided.*" Just because you believe in divine protection doesn't mean you can go anywhere, do anything, and always be guaranteed protection.

I remember one time when I was a student at Oral Roberts University, I asked a senior if he knew what he was going to do after graduation. He told me that he was going to travel around the world as a missionary. I said, "That's great that you heard from God that He has called you to be a missionary." He responded, "Oh, I never heard God call me to be a missionary. I'm just going because Jesus said that we are to spread the gospel around the world."

I don't know if this man and his wife ever did go on the mission field. However, I hope if he and his wife did, they truly sought the Lord first before going to any nation. It is vital for you to hear from God first to know that you are in the right place at the right time. You want to make sure the Lord is leading you when you are depending on Him for protection. You need to have both His protection and His wisdom.

Paul and his companions were led by the Holy Spirit throughout their missionary travels. When Paul, Silas, and Luke tried to go to Asia, the Holy Spirit would not allow them, "Now when they had gone through Phrygia and the region of Galatia, they were forbidden by the Holy Spirit to preach the word in Asia" (Acts 16:6). When they attempted to preach the gospel in Bithynia, the Holy Spirit did not let them go there either: "After they had come to Mysia, they tried to go in Bithynia, but the Spirit did not permit them" (Acts 16:7).

The Holy Spirit led the disciples and prevented them from going to places where they would have endangered their lives. Had the disciples not obeyed the promptings and guidance of the Holy Spirit, it is most probable that they would have lost their lives because they were out of the will of God. The Holy Spirit provided wisdom, which guarded them from premature death. Paul and his companions surely understood these words from Proverbs:

> *Trust in the LORD with all your heart, and lean not on your own understanding; in all your ways acknowledge Him, and He shall direct your paths.*

Proverbs 3:5-6

> *My son, let them not depart from your eyes—keep sound wisdom and discretion; so they will be life to your soul and grace to your neck. Then you will walk safely in your way, and your foot will not stumble.*

Proverbs 3:21-23

"Cancel the Meeting"

When I was starting out in ministry twenty-five years ago, I would preach during the summer at local churches. I traveled from city to city holding what we called "revival services." At the end of one summer, I was invited to a church to hold a week-long revival service. At the time, I especially was excited for the opportunity and the financial support since I was a student at Oral Roberts University. The local pastor had arranged a place for me to stay and was going to take care of all my expenses. I was so glad about the opportunity, but something inside me felt wrong. I kept hearing His voice inside me saying, "You need to cancel the meeting." I just sensed that something was not right. I had no peace inside, but I kept overriding the promptings. As I drove toward the city, I became more and more aware that I was not in the will of God. I felt upset and uneasy because I knew that I was not supposed to have the meetings.

Have you ever had this happen? Have you ever tried to change God's mind since you were bound and determined to have your way? That's what I did. I argued with God, and that is never a good idea. I kept telling Him the reason He needed to change His mind and why He needed to agree with me, "You know, Lord, that I need the money! And not only that, I can't just tell the pastor to cancel these services! That wouldn't be right of me."

The closer I came to the city where the meetings were to be held, the more I felt troubled inside. As I drove into town, I saw a sign welcoming me to the city. As soon as my car passed the sign and entered into the city...*WHAM*! A car hit me from behind and sent me flying off the road. When the driver who hit me got out of her car, it was immediately apparent she was as drunk as a skunk. She screamed at me, "What were you doing? Why were you in my way? This is all your fault! I'm gonna call the police!" As soon as the police arrived, they arrested her. (Not surprisingly, I learned this was not her first arrest for DWI - driving while intoxicated.) The meetings ended up getting canceled and the pastor graciously blessed me with an offering. I went back to school with a learned lesson and aching whiplash.

When I got to the dormitory, I said to the Lord, "You warned me and I should have listened and followed Your voice. I repent. Thank You Lord for protecting me in the accident. I forgive the lady who hit me. I receive Your forgiveness and I receive my healing in Jesus' name." The very moment I prayed and received the Lord's forgiveness, I also received His healing. I never had any pain in my neck ever again. Thank the Lord for His goodness and His mercy. You will never go wrong when you listen and obey God's voice. He will never lead you into misfortune, but will always lead you away from trouble and into all truth.

Whoever Listens to Me

It pays to hear the voice of the Lord, and it costs you when you ignore His voice. The Lord warned Israel that when they despised His counsel, they would not live in His secret place of protection. In the past, Israel had suffered calamity and destruction for their complacency.

> *Because they hated knowledge and did not choose the fear of the LORD, they would have none of my counsel and despised my every rebuke. Therefore they shall eat the fruit of their own way, and be filled to the full with their own fancies. For the turning away of the simple will slay them, and the complacency of fools will destroy them; but whoever listens to me will dwell safely, and will be secure, without fear of evil.*

> Proverbs 1:29-33

Notice the one who listens and receives God's counsel will be secure, without the fear of evil. Those who do not turn away from their own complacency will be slain and destroyed. In the past, Israel had lost respect and honor for the Lord. As a result, they reaped destruction and captivity. They did not honor God, which caused them to suffer misfortune.

> *Those who respect [fear] the LORD will have security [or confidence], and their children will be protected [have a refuge]. Respect for [Fear of] the LORD gives life [is a fountain of life] and can save people from death [turning people aside from death traps/snares].*

Proverbs 14:26-27, EXB

The fear of the LORD leads to life, and he who has it will abide in satisfaction; he will not be visited with evil.

Proverbs 19:23

Boasting of Tomorrow

Do not boast about tomorrow, for you do not know what a day may bring forth.

Proverbs 27:1

What you say about tomorrow needs to agree with God's Word and His wisdom. When you boast about your own ideas, your own plans, your own agenda, then you are leaving the Lord out of tomorrow and relying on your own wisdom and strength.

Listen to counsel and receive instruction, that you may be wise in your latter days. There are many plans in a man's heart, nevertheless the LORD's counsel – that will stand.

Proverbs 19:20-21

Look to the Lord to guard over your life. "Unless the LORD builds the house, they labor in vain who build it; unless the LORD guards the city, the watchman stays awake in vain" (Psalm 127:1). When you boast in your own strength and wisdom, you are foolishly treating life as if you have full control.

Someone may boast in arrogance, "I don't need Jesus as a crutch. I live in a safe neighborhood. And besides that, I always keep my weapons ready and loaded just in case someone wants to mess with me!" This person's trust is in their own strength and resources. The problem with that is their own strength and resources will never be enough to keep them and their family safe in these perilous times.

A Taser in your purse cannot protect your children while they are away from you. Jiu jitsu lessons cannot help you when a stray bullet is coming toward your head. Your safe driving skills cannot prevent an intoxicated driver from flying through a traffic light and crashing into your car. You and your family need supernatural protection 24/7 in these last days.

You do not want to be caught being wise in your own eyes. The wisdom of God and the fear of the Lord will always lead you into paths of shalom and out of paths of catastrophe.

> *Happy is the man who finds wisdom, and the man who gains understanding; for her proceeds are better than the profits of silver, and her gain than fine gold. She is more precious than rubies, and all the things you may desire cannot compare with her. Length of days is in her right hand, in her left hand riches and honor. Her ways are ways of pleasantness, and all her paths are peace. She is a tree of life to those who take hold of her, and happy are all who retain her.*

> Proverbs 3:13-18

If someone says, "Tomorrow, I am going to do such and such," but ignores the wisdom of God in the matter, he is being careless and even foolish. He may think to himself, "I've always been able to take care of myself. What will happen, will happen. It is what it is!" That person lacks the wisdom of God. He is wise in his own eyes.

You have no idea what you will face tomorrow. Everything you do needs to be based on the wisdom of God and the leading of the Spirit.

> *Come now, you who say, "Today or tomorrow we will go to such and such a city, spend a year there, buy and sell,*

*and make a profit"; whereas you do not know what will
happen tomorrow...Instead you ought to say, "If the Lord
wills, we shall live and do this or that." But now you boast
in your arrogance. All such boasting is evil.*

James 4:13-16

Does the Lord will for you to live tomorrow? Of course He
does. He guarantees long life when you follow His voice of
wisdom (Proverbs 3:16). However, tomorrow is only guaranteed
when you are walking in His wisdom. When you acknowledge
Him in all your ways, He will direct your path (Proverbs 3:6).
When you make plans for tomorrow, you should always check
inside for the counsel of the Holy Spirit. Do you have a peace?
Are you being led by the Spirit? It is vital for you to learn how to
be led by the Spirit and not just make decisions based on what
makes sense to you. God sees things ahead that you don't see.

When you boast in your own wisdom and disregard the wisdom
of God, your life can appear as a vapor and suddenly vanish away.
Don't make decisions based on your own wisdom. Base your
decisions on the Lord's wisdom. We have all made dumb
mistakes that have cost us dearly. Every one of us needs to hear
and yield to the voice of God's wisdom on a daily basis.

The Inside Counselor

Don't be afraid that you will not be able to hear God's voice.
As a believer, you have the Holy Spirit inside your heart and you
have the ability to hear Him: "The sheep that are My own hear and
are listening to My voice; and I know them, and they follow me"
(John 10:27, AMPC).

The Holy Spirit is your inside counselor. He abides inside your
heart and will teach you how to stay safely under the shadow of
the Almighty. He will guide you into all truth.

But the Comforter (Counselor, Helper, Intercessor, Advocate, Strengthener, Standby), the Holy Spirit, Whom the Father will send in My name [in My place, to represent Me and act on My behalf], He will teach you all things.

John 14:26, AMPC

But you have an anointing from the Holy One, and you know all things.

1 John 2:20

But the anointing which you have received from Him abides in you, and you do not need that anyone teach you; but as the same anointing teaches you concerning all things, and is true, and is not a lie, and just as it has taught you, you will abide in Him.

1 John 2:27

"Don't Go!"

My wife could have been in a serious car accident had she not heeded to the voice of the Spirit. One day, Lena was waiting at a traffic light. When the light turned green, she heard in her heart, "Don't go." Rather than ignore the warning, she yielded to the inward voice. She sat at the green light and waited a few seconds. All of a sudden, a car came flying through the red light and would have crashed into the driver's side of her car had she accelerated. What did Lena do to prevent a serious car accident? She heard and yielded to the voice of the Spirit, the voice of wisdom. "A man's heart plans his way, but the LORD directs his steps" (Proverbs 16:9).

When the voice of the Holy Spirit tells you, "Slow down," what should you do? Ignore it? Reason it away as your imagination? That is how we get into trouble and even dangerous situations - we disregard the inward witness. Hearing and yielding to the voice of the Spirit is vital.

Wisdom Cries Aloud

Wisdom cries aloud in the street, she raises her voice in the markets; she cries at the head of the noisy intersections [in the chief gathering places]; at the entrance of the city gates she speaks.

Proverbs 1:20-21, AMPC

Notice that the voice of wisdom cries, raises her voice, and speaks. The question is – are we listening? Sometimes we get so busy that we are not in tune to hearing wisdom's voice. The voice of wisdom will speak to you in the marketplace, at the shopping mall, and even while you are driving downtown in heavy traffic.

Turn at my rebuke; surely I will pour out my spirit on you; I will make my words known to you.

Proverbs 1:23

But whoever listens to me will dwell safely, and will be secure, without fear of evil.

Proverbs 1:33

Notice that wisdom does not just speak to you at the altar or in your prayer closet. There are people who have avoided tragedy because they heard the voice of wisdom cry out in their spirit, "Stay home. Do not go downtown today," or "Do not take this airline flight," or "Take your children to school; don't let them take the bus." This is not the voice of fear or paranoia but the voice of the Holy Spirit who will guide you into all truth (John 16:13). When you hear His voice, simply follow Him and trust in His leadership.

Road Rage Averted

When I drive on the highway, I keep watch in my heart for the Lord's wisdom and direction. This is especially important driving on the roads of South Florida, which are known to be some of the most dangerous places to drive in the United States. One day I was driving on the highway and I heard the voice of the Holy Spirit say, "Slow down! Pray Psalm 91!" As I began to pray Psalm 91, suddenly two cars came flying past me and crashed into each other in front of my car. This was an obvious act of "road rage," two raging mad drivers crashing into each other. Smoke and fragments of the cars came soaring toward me, but I drove through the accident untouched.

The Holy Spirit warned me. God knew what was up ahead, but I had to hear His voice. What would have happened had I not heard or yielded to His voice? What if I would have rationalized it away and thought, *There is no need to slow down. I'm already running late*? Had I ignored the voice of the Holy Spirit, I could have been in a major car accident.

I am so thankful for the Holy Spirit and for the fact that I am never alone. The Holy Spirit lives on the inside of you. He is always with you and will direct your steps out of harm's way. He will lead you into all truth so you'll make wise decisions. Anytime you hear the voice of the Holy Spirit about anything, you always need to make sure you listen and follow His voice. His voice will lead you into "paths of peace" (Proverbs 3:17). When you don't have a peace inside, don't take the path!

CHAPTER 15

SHALOM ON YOUR HOME

Jesus appointed seventy of His disciples to go out and preach the good news in the cities of Israel (Luke 10:1). He wanted those seventy to be totally dependent upon the Father for both provision and protection. He instructed the disciples not to carry any money bag, knapsack, or sandals and not to greet anyone along the road (Luke 10:4). Why would Jesus specifically tell His disciples not to greet anyone along the road? He wanted to ensure that the first words the disciples spoke when they entered an area were, "Shalom to this house" (Luke 10:5). The members of the household would either receive the blessing of shalom or reject it. Jesus stated that if they received the blessing of shalom, they would continue in peace and safety. If they rejected it, then the blessing of shalom would return back to the disciple who declared it (Luke 10:6).

The Blessing of Shalom

When the seventy returned, they were filled with joy testifying of the many supernatural signs that followed them. Pronouncing shalom over each house caused supernatural power to be released, even making demons subject to the name of Jesus (Luke 10:17). Jesus responded to His disciples' reports by sharing how He saw Satan fall to earth like lightning striking the ground (Luke 10:18). Jesus then gave His disciples a promise of divine protection, "Behold, I give you the authority to trample on serpents and scorpions, and over all the power of the enemy, and nothing shall by any means hurt you" (Luke 10:19).

This promise to the believers is in agreement with Psalm 91, which also says the Lord will protect His people from all the power of the enemy and gives them authority to tread on the enemy: "No evil shall befall you, nor shall any plague come near your dwelling" (Psalm 91:10). The promises found in Luke 10:19 and Psalm 91:10 agree that the believer has divine protection.

It is not your "lot in life" to have discord and chaos in your city or neighborhood. God's shalom is available to you and your entire family, regardless whether you live in a rural area, the suburbs, or in the inner city. When you confess God's Word of protection over your family, home, car, school, movie theatre, on your vacation, in a hotel - wherever you may be going that day - the blessing of shalom will be manifested. When you pronounce the blessing of shalom, you are releasing God's power for peace and protection.

Esther's Decree

No matter where you live, that is your place of dominion. You have been given the promise of shalom for your neighborhood, your city, and your nation. It doesn't matter how poor, violent, or evil your surroundings may be, you are to bring shalom to that place.

The book of Esther is a detailed narrative, telling how the Lord kept Israel safe in dangerous times by using a young Jewish woman named Hadassah. (Later on her name was changed to "Esther," which means "star.") A unique feature of the book of

Esther is the absence of the name of God. Esther is the only book in the Bible in which the name of God is never mentioned. Why would this book not mention the name of God? Possibly it is because during the time when Israel was under the rule of the Persian Empire, the name of God was not allowed to be mentioned.

When the story of Esther takes place, the Israelites had been free to return to Jerusalem for over fifty years, but many of them still lived in Babylon under Persian rule (Ezra 1:2). Haman, the chief minister, was second in command to the king of Persia. Haman's anger and hatred toward the Jews and Esther's uncle Mordecai in particular, inspired him to get permission from the king to slaughter all the Jews. Esther, the queen of Persia who happened to be Jewish, was warned by her uncle Mordecai of Haman's plot. Esther fasted and prayed for three days in preparation for her appearance before the king of Persia.

> *So it was, when the king saw Queen Esther standing in the court, that she found favor in his sight.*

> Esther 5:2

Esther warned the king of Haman's conspiracy to wipe out the Jewish population and the king had Haman hanged on the very gallows Haman constructed for the death of Mordecai (Esther 7). But unfortunately, the king's decree to allow for the annihilation of the Jews could not be overturned since Persian law made any formal edict from the king irrevocable. The king did allow Esther to write a decree giving the Jews authorization to protect themselves from all their enemies and he allows her to seal it with the king's royal seal (Esther 8:7-8).

> *By these letters the king permitted the Jews who were in every city to gather together and protect their lives – to*

destroy, kill, and annihilate all the forces of any people or province that would assault them, both little children and women, and to plunder their possessions.

Esther 8:11

Esther's bold decree prompted many people from the surrounding cities and states to become Jewish: "The Jews had light and gladness, joy and honor. And in every province and city, wherever the king's command and decree came, the Jews had joy and gladness, a feast and a holiday. Then many of the people of the land became Jews, because fear of the Jews fell upon them" (Esther 8:16-17).

All those who hated the Jews and desired to wipe them out were slaughtered by the armed Jewish people, "Thus the Jews defeated all their enemies with the stroke of the sword, with slaughter and destruction, and did what they pleased with those who hated them" (Esther 9:5). The number of those enemies of the Jews who were killed was recorded as more than 75,000. "The remainder of the Jews in the king's provinces gathered together and protected their lives, had rest from their enemies and killed seventy-five thousand of their enemies; but they did not lay a hand on the plunder" (Esther 9:16).

The Jewish people were instructed to commemorate God's divine protection and deliverance with the celebration of the Feast of Purim, which is still celebrated today by Jews everywhere (Esther 9:20-23). Esther received divine favor, which brought divine protection to her people. The Jews were given rest from their enemies after they rose up and defended themselves. They were able to lead quiet lives of shalom. The blessing of shalom is intended not only for your home, but also for your nation.

That We May Lead a Quiet and Peaceable Life

The National Day of Prayer is observed on the first Thursday of May each year. Presidents George W. Bush, Barak Obama, and

Donald Trump requested the Lord's divine protection in their National Day of Prayer proclamations.

> "Now, therefore, I George W. Bush, President of the United States of America, do hereby proclaim May 1, 2008, as a National Day of Prayer. I ask the citizens of our Nation to give thanks...for God's continued guidance, comfort, and protection." [41]

> "Now, therefore, I Barack Obama, President of the United States...do hereby proclaim May 5, 2016, as National Day of Prayer...I join all people of faith in asking for God's continued guidance, mercy, and protection as we seek a more just world." [42]

> "Now, therefore, I, Donald J. Trump, President of the United States of America...do hereby proclaim May 4, 2017, as a National Day of Prayer. I invite the citizens of our Nation to pray, in accordance with their own faiths and consciences, in thanksgiving for the freedoms and blessings we have received, and for God's guidance and continued protection as we meet the challenges before us." [43]

The apostle Paul addressed the subject of submitting to governing authorities. He admonished the Church to honor and submit to those who bear the sword for executing justice against those who do evil (Romans 13:3-4) and referred to those governing authorities as being "appointed by God" (Romans 13:1), "God's minister to you for good" (Romans 13:4), and "God's minister, an avenger to execute wrath on him who practices evil" (Romans 13:4). The police and military are not just working for the government, they are ordained by God to do good and provide protection.

Modern day authorities would include all civil officers, state, county, police, and military forces. Paul instructed Timothy to offer up prayers for those in authority, "Therefore I exhort first of all that supplications, prayers, intercessions, and giving of thanks be made for all men, for kings and all who are in authority, that we may lead a quiet and peaceable life in all godliness and reverence" (1 Timothy 2:1-2). Notice that when you pray for those who are in authority over your community, city, and nation, you will experience "a quiet and peaceable life" - the blessing of shalom. The peace and safety of shalom will surround your city, neighborhood, and nation as you daily cover the authorities with God's blood covenant of divine protection.

It is vital for the Church to make supplications, prayers, intercessions, and giving of thanks for those in authority. This does not mean that your prayers will create "world peace." Jesus made it clear that in the last days there would be wars and chaos, but we are not to be troubled.

> *And you will hear of wars and rumors of wars. See that you are not troubled; for all these things must come to pass, but the end is not yet. For nation will rise against nation, and kingdom against kingdom. And there will be famines, pestilences, and earthquakes in various places.*

> Matthew 24:6-7

When Jesus says, "See that you are not troubled," it is not a suggestion but a command. Jesus provides His shalom to make it possible. You can have His peace in the midst of a world filled with chaos and stress.

> *Peace I leave with you. My peace I give to you; not as the world gives do I give to you. Let not your heart be troubled, neither let it be afraid.*

> John 14:27

You may think it's impossible to not be troubled by all the devastation and danger that is in the world. The fact is, it is impossible when you are outside the shadow of the Almighty. That is why you must keep the Word of God in front of your eyes and in your ears and coming out of your mouth daily. Spend time in the Lord's presence worshipping Him and in return, you'll receive His joy and peace. Don't let a day go by without covering you and your family with the blood of Jesus. Keep the promises of protection overflowing in your heart and coming from your mouth. You will experience shalom on your home as you dwell safely underneath His wings of protection.

PRAYER OF PROTECTION

Take the blood covenant of divine protection and verbally declare these things by faith.

In the name of Jesus, I cover myself, my spouse, my children, every member of my family, all my possessions, my church, my friends, my neighborhood, my city, and the nation's governing authority with the blood of Jesus.

I declare that we dwell in the secret place of the Most High. We abide under the shadow of the Almighty. I will say of the Lord, He is our refuge and our fortress; He is our God, and in Him we will trust.

Surely He shall deliver us from the snare of the fowler and from the perilous pestilence. He shall cover us with His feathers, and under His wings we shall take refuge; His truth is our shield and buckler.

We shall not be afraid of the terror by night, nor of the arrow that flies by day, nor of the pestilence that walks in darkness, nor of the destruction that lays waste at noonday.

A thousand may fall at our side, and ten thousand at our right hand; but it shall not come near us. Only with our eyes we shall look, and see the reward of the wicked.

Because we have made the Lord who is our refuge, even the Most High, our dwelling place, no evil shall befall us, nor shall any plague come near our dwelling;

for He shall give His angels charge over us, to keep us in all our ways. In their hands they shall bear us up, lest we dash our foot against a stone.

We shall tread upon the lion and the cobra, the young lion and the serpent we shall trample underfoot.

Because we have set our love upon Him, therefore He will deliver us; He will set us on high, because we know His name.

We shall call upon Him, and He will answer us; He will be with us in trouble and will deliver us and honor us. With long life He will satisfy us, and show us His salvation.

Amen.

- Psalm 91, paraphrased

FINAL WORDS

I pray that this book has helped you receive a fresh revelation and understanding of your inheritance of divine protection in Christ Jesus. It is an honor for me to share these truths with you.

As you abide in the secret place of the Most High, you will experience the supernatural protection of the blood covenant.

I would love to hear about your experience and look forward to receiving your testimonies of supernatural protection. You can contact our ministry by visiting our website at **harvesti.org**.

May God's grace and shalom be multiplied to you and your entire family, in Jesus' name. Amen.

PRAYER OF SALVATION

No one has been made right before God through their own efforts. Everyone has sinned and fallen short of God's standards of perfection: "For all have sinned and fall short of the glory of God" (Romans 3:23). Jesus is the only one who fully and perfectly fulfilled all the requirements of the law. You are not right with God because of any righteous acts you have done; He considers them like filthy rags covered in human blood (Isaiah 64:6). The only way you can be right with God is to accept His free gift of righteousness through faith in the blood of His Son, Jesus: "Therefore, having been justified by faith, we have peace with God through our Lord Jesus Christ" (Romans 5:1).

If you have never called on Jesus to be your Lord and Savior, today is the day of salvation. I invite you to pray this prayer aloud from your heart:

Jesus, I am a sinner and I am in need of a Savior.

I believe You are the Son of God. I believe You died on the cross and shed Your blood for me.

I believe God raised You from the dead. I believe You are seated at His right hand in heaven.

I receive Your forgiveness of all my sins.

God, You are my Father.

Jesus, You are my Lord and Savior.

Holy Spirit, You live on the inside of me. Fill me with Your power as I yield myself to You.

In Jesus' name, Amen!

ABOUT THE AUTHOR

For over twenty-five years, Dr. Miltenberger has been preaching and teaching the Word of God with the demonstration of the power of the Holy Spirit in church services, conferences, Bible schools, radio, youth ministry, outreaches, and prisons.

His messages of faith declare that God is good and there is supernatural power in the Word, the Name, and the Blood of Jesus.

Dr. Miltenberger is the founder of Harvest International with the calling to reach the unreached, to tell the untold, to go where the light of the gospel is seen only dimly.

Brian, his wife Lena, and their two children Joshua and Hannah, live in South Florida.

For more information about the ministry outreach of Harvest International please visit **harvesti.org**.

PROTECTION

NOTES

Chapter One

James Strong. *Exhaustive Concordance of the Bible* (Peabody, Massachusetts: Hendrickson Publishers, 2009), Strong's Number 7965.

W.E. Vine. *Vine's Complete Expository Dictionary of the Old Testament Words* (Nashville, Tennessee: Thomas Nelson Publishers, 1985), 173.

Chapter Two

[2] *Chabad.org*; "The Complete Jewish Bible with Rashi Commentary: Tehillim – Psalms – Chapter 91," comment on verse 1, http://www.chabad.org/library/bible_cdo/aid/16312/jewish/Chapter-91.htm#showrashi=true.

Charles H. Spurgeon, "Psalm 91 Bible Commentary," *Treasury of David,* http://www.christianity.com/bible/commentary.php?com=spur.

[3] James Strong. *Exhaustive Concordance of the Bible* (Peabody, Massachusetts: Hendrickson Publishers, 2009), Strong's Number 4583.

[4] Ibid., Strong's Number 3427.

[5] Ibid., Strong's Number 3885.

[6] Note from *The Spirit Filled Life Study Bible (SFB). New King James Version* (Nashville, Tennessee: Thomas Nelson Publishers, 1991), 753.

Chapter Three

[7] James Strong. *Exhaustive Concordance of the Bible* (Peabody, Massachusetts: Hendrickson Publishers, 2009), Strong's Number 4268.

[8] Ibid., Strong's Number 6738.

Chapter Four

[9] Lucy Kinder, "13 of the most unusual phobias," *The Telegraph*, September 6, 2013, http://www.telegraph.co.uk/news/science/10289366/13-of-the-most-unusual-phobias.html.

[10] H.A. Maxwell Whyte. *The Power of the Blood* (New Kensington, Pennsylvania: Whitaker House, 1973), 23.

[11] M. James Freeman. *Manners and Customs of the Bible* (Plainfield, New Jersey: Logos International, 1972), 179.

Chapter Five

[12] James Strong. *Exhaustive Concordance of the Bible* (Peabody, Massachusetts: Hendrickson Publishers, 2009), Strong's Number 8104.

[13] Ibid., Strong's Number 7965.

[14] *The Complete Biblical Library: Volume 6: Study Bible, Acts* (Springfield, Missouri: The Complete Biblical Library, 1986), 637.

[15] Ibid., 641.

[16] Ibid., 643.

[17] Madeline S. Miller and J. Lane Miller. *Harper's Bible Dictionary* (New York, New York: Harper & Row Publishers, 1973), 797.

Chapter Six

[18] Note associated with John 18:3 in *The Amplified Bible.*

[19] Genesis 16:7-8; 19:1; Numbers 22:31; Judges 6:11-13; 13:6; 2 Samuel 24:16; 1 Chronicles 21:15; Daniel 3:28; 6:22; Hosea 12:4; Zechariah 1:18; 3:4; 4:6; 5:5-6; Matthew 25:41; 28:1-4; Luke 1:19; 1:26; 24:4; Acts 12:7; Jude 6-9; Revelation 9:1; 9:11; 10:1; 12:7-9; 14:17-19; 16:3-17; 20:1; 21:17; 22:8-10

[20] Psalm 104:4; Zechariah 6:5-8; Acts 23:8; Hebrews 1:7

[21] Exodus 3:2; 14:19, 24; Judges 13:19-21; 2 Kings 6:17; Psalm 104:4; Acts 7:30; Hebrews 1:7 Revelation 10:1; 19:17

Chapter Seven

[22] James Strong. *Exhaustive Concordance of the Bible* (Peabody, Massachusetts: Hendrickson Publishers, 2009), Strong's Number 7429.

[23] Note from *The Spirit Filled Life Study Bible (SFB), New King James Version* (Nashville, Tennessee: Thomas Nelson Publishers, 1991), 1240.

Chapter Eight

[24] Joan Comay and Ronald Brownrigg. *Who's Who In the Bible: Two Volumes in One* (New York, New York: Bonanza Books, 1980), 69.

Chapter Nine

[25] John MacArthur. *The MacArthur Bible Commentary.* (Nashville, Tennessee: Thomas Nelson Publishers, 2005), 87.

[26] Joan Comay and Ronald Brownrigg. *Who's Who In the Bible: Two Volumes in One* (New York, New York: Bonanza Books, 1980), 235.

[27] W.E. Vine. *Vine's Complete Expository Dictionary of the Old Testament Words* (Nashville, Tennessee: Thomas Nelson Publishers, 1985), 333.

[28] John MacArthur. *The MacArthur New Testament Commentary: Matthew 8-15* (Chicago, Illinois: The Moody Bible Institute of Chicago, 1987), 32.

Chapter Ten

[29] Note from *The Spirit Filled Life Study Bible (SFB). New King James Version* (Nashville, Tennessee: Thomas Nelson Publishers, 1991), 1700.

Chapter Eleven

[30] James Strong. *Exhaustive Concordance of the Bible* (Peabody, Massachusetts: Hendrickson Publishers, 2009), Strong's Number 3444.

[31] Ibid., 726.

Chapter Twelve

[32] Joan Comay and Ronald Brownrigg. *Who's Who In the Bible: Two Volumes in One* (New York, New York: Bonanza Books, 1980), 147.

[33] Ibid., 267.

[34] Ibid., 60.

Chapter Thirteen

[35] W.E. Vine. *Vine's Complete Expository Dictionary of the Old Testament Words* (Nashville, Tennessee: Thomas Nelson Publishers, 1985), 18.

[36] James Strong. *Exhaustive Concordance of the Bible* (Peabody, Massachusetts: Hendrickson Publishers, 2009), Strong's Number 7753.

[37] Note from *The Spirit Filled Life Study Bible (SFB). New King James Version* (Nashville, Tennessee: Thomas Nelson Publishers, 1991), 710.

[38] James Strong. *Exhaustive Concordance of the Bible* (Peabody, Massachusetts: Hendrickson Publishers, 2009), Strong's Number 8104.

[39] Ibid.

[40] Ibid., Strong's Number 7965.

Chapter Fifteen

[41] "National Day of Prayer, 2008," *whitehouse.gov*, April 22, 2008, https://georgewbush-whitehouse.archives.gov/news/releases/2008/04/20080422-6.html.

[42] "Presidential Proclamation – National Day of Prayer, 2016," *whitehouse.gov*, May 4, 2016, https://obamawhitehouse.archives.gov/the-press-office/2016/05/04/presidential-proclamation-national-day-prayer-2016.

[43] "President Donald J. Trump Proclaims May 4, 2017, as a National Day of Prayer," *whitehouse.gov*, May 4, 2017, https://www.whitehouse.gov/the-press-office/2017/05/04/president-donald-j-trump-proclaims

Made in the USA
Lexington, KY
03 January 2019